WILLIAMS-SONOMA

New American Cooking

New England

GENERAL EDITOR **Chuck Williams**

RECIPES AND TEXT **Molly Stevens**

FOOD PHOTOGRAPHY **Leigh Beisch**

TIME
LIFE
BOOKS

New Ameri

The Pacific Northwest

California

The Southwest

an Cooking

Heartland

New England

The South

Table of **Contents**

Introduction

I first came to New England in the late 1970s as a college student and have lived, on and off, in the region ever since. During this time, I have eaten my way around the towns and villages, big cities and rural outposts, seaside resorts and woodland camps of my adopted home. I have shared meals in welcoming homes, at community suppers, at county fairs, in roadside diners, and in first-class restaurants. So when I set out to catalog the contemporary cuisine of this diverse region, I figured it would be a simple matter of retracing my steps.

What I quickly learned, however, is that much of the time New Englanders eat like the rest of America thanks to the inescapable spread of food trends. At the same time, I discovered that the real soul of New England cooking today is best defined by the zeal that home cooks and chefs express for their bounty of local, seasonal ingredients.

This book does not attempt to survey all of the dishes served in the region. Rather it reflects the foods, recipes, and ways of cooking that distinguish New England from the rest of the country. Thus, along with presenting such iconographic New England dishes as chowder, pot roast, and bread pudding, this collection explores the vibrant palette of the region's contemporary cuisine. At the same time, it paints a lively portrait of the eclectic mix of foods and people that sets the Northeast apart.

The Lay of the Land

New England is the smallest, most compact region in the country. Altogether, the six states—Maine, New Hampshire, Vermont, Massachusetts, Rhode Island, and Connecticut—that make up the area could fit easily into Missouri with ample room to spare. Despite the condensed layout, one of the most remarkable aspects is the diverse geography punctuated by a craggy seacoast, vast inland waterways, rugged mountains, sleepy pastoral towns, sprawling urban centers, hilly pastures, wide river valleys, and a patchwork of productive farmland.

The dense northern woodlands, which stretch from the Longfellow Mountains of northern Maine, across the White Mountains of New Hampshire, and all the way to the Green Mountains of Vermont, provide a bounty of game—small and large—including venison, moose, pheasant, partridge, wild turkey, and grouse.

The sugar maple dominates many of these forests as well. The production of maple syrup and its use in any number of both savory and sweet recipes is testament to its eminence.

Probably the most renowned geographical feature of New England is the seacoast that reaches from the Long Island Sound, out and around the crooked arm of Cape Cod, and all the way north to the Canadian border and beyond. From the cold waters of the Atlantic comes a great variety of seafood, including lobster, haddock, bass, hake, pollack, cod, mackerel, swordfish, tuna, flounder, herring, clams, oysters, and mussels.

In addition to the woodlands and seacoast, much of the region remains in farmland. The richest soil is found in the Connecticut River Valley, which defines the border between New Hampshire and Vermont and extends down through western Massachusetts and Connecticut. Traditionally, dairy farming has been the primary livelihood in this fertile valley, and, as a result, milk, cream, and cheese are key ingredients in many farmhouse recipes, such as milk-based soups and gravies, gratins, scalloped dishes, ice creams, and custard pies.

Over the past several decades, however, the face of farming in the region has been changing. The number of small-scale specialty farming operations that emphasize organic and sustainable practices is growing and making a profound contribution to the culinary landscape. A wide range of such products have enjoyed success, including sheep's milk cheese from Shepherd's in Vermont, organic lamb from Foxfire Farm in Connecticut, and heirloom potatoes from Wood Prairie Farm in Maine. These are just a few of the high-quality regional products that find their way to the farmers' markets and local stores and onto restaurant menus.

The Hands That Stir the Pots

Although the region was first settled by the Pilgrims, the contemporary character of New England cooking owes much to the variety of populations that have immigrated here over the centuries. In the north, large communities of French Canadians make their pea soup, terrines, and cured meats. The Italians came to work the granite quarries in northern Vermont, and they also established thriving communities in New Haven and in Boston's North End. Descendants of Scotch and Welsh immigrants populate Maine, New Hampshire, and Vermont, adding lamb stews and oat breads to the mix. German settlers brought a taste for sausages and cabbage to Maine. The

New England provides the country with a stunning array of oysters, including the Wellfleets and Belons suggested for a festive stew (opposite). Savoy cabbage (above) is delicious in an updated version of the signature New England Boiled Dinner (page 74).

11

Home of the first American apple trees, New England continues to produce many varieties of apples (above), including Rhode Island Greening and Northern Spy. A seafood grill (right) highlights the diversity of fish and shellfish harvested in the region. New England, long renowned for its delicious Vermont cheddar, also produces several excellent artisan cheeses (opposite) such as varieties of goat and blue.

Portuguese fishermen adopted their traditional foods to the climate of southern Massachusetts and Rhode Island. The Irish are synonymous with the character of Boston's politics and spirit. And today, Asians, Bosnians, Greeks, Lebanese, Poles, and Hungarians have added an enticing array of ingredients, flavorings, and recipes to the regional cuisine.

A Rich Tradition

It is impossible to look at the contemporary cooking of New England without discussing the role that tradition plays. Like that of the South, the cooking of New England has deep roots in the colonial foods of early America. Although the cooking has evolved over the centuries, change doesn't come easily in Yankee kitchens, and many cooks and diners still favor recipes handed down from their grandmothers. In farm kitchens in northern New Hampshire, chipped beef with milk gravy remains a favorite evening meal, and at Durgin Park in Boston's Quincy

Market, baked beans are served just as they were 150 years ago.

Despite such modern comforts as central heating and polar fleece clothing, there's not a single New Englander who doesn't deal with the reality of the harsh, often long northern winters (with the exception of those retired part-timers we call "snow birds," who migrate to Florida as soon as the first flakes fly). The familiarity with cold weather manifests itself in a sumptuous repertoire of hearty dishes that includes chowders, soups, and stews—all typically made from a base of onions cooked in pork fat or butter.

Evidence of the early hardscrabble life in such a severe climate and of the religious austerity of the Puritan forefathers is still seen in the archetypal grizzled, wool-clad, fiercely independent Yankee character. While this image has softened over the years, and fewer and fewer individuals are scratching out a living in uninsulated farmhouses miles from the nearest phone, there remains something palpable about the Yankee spirit that translates into the food of the region. Yankee cooks are still mostly conservative and frugal. Meals are simple, often composed of a few good-quality ingredients and served in large portions. Flavors are deep and satisfying, not needing a lot of fancy adornments or much trendy flair.

In the end, the food of the region reflects a vibrant mix of traditional and modern tastes with a deep connection to the land and to the sea. The varied landscape, the dramatic seasonal changes, and the diversity of the inhabitants all contribute to the rich culinary feast that is New England.

1 Starters, Soups & Salads

As a rule, New Englanders don't much care to categorize their recipes according to when and how to eat a certain dish. Instead, dishes are served in different guises according to the season and the appetite. A plate of hot johnnycakes, for example, may be a filling, cold-weather breakfast or the start of an elegant dinner—or it may be the whole meal. The following recipes for starters, soups, and salads can be served as openers to more expansive meals or on their own as satisfying lunches, suppers, or even breakfasts if you've got a big day ahead of you.

Rhode Island Johnnycakes with Country Ham

1½ cups (7½ oz/235 g) white or yellow cornmeal, preferably stone-ground

1 teaspoon salt

1 teaspoon sugar

1½ cups (12 fl oz/375 ml) boiling water

1 small yellow onion, grated (about ⅓ cup/2 oz/60 g)

¼–½ cup (2–4 fl oz/60–125 ml) milk

½ cup (3 oz/90 g) finely chopped country ham

freshly ground pepper to taste

2–3 tablespoons unsalted butter

Cornmeal pancakes are popular throughout New England, but nowhere are they taken as seriously as they are in Rhode Island. This savory adaptation makes a wonderful hors d'oeuvre or starter served plain or topped with a dollop of crème fraîche flavored with red onions, roasted garlic, or chives.

1. Preheat the oven to 200°F (95°C).

2. In a bowl, using a wooden spoon, stir together the cornmeal, salt, and sugar. Slowly stir in the boiling water, mixing until smooth and quite stiff. Let the batter stand for 5 minutes.

3. Stir in the grated onion. Add enough of the milk to make a batter the consistency of porridge. Stir in the ham and season with pepper.

4. Preheat a griddle or frying pan, preferably nonstick, over medium heat. Add about ½ tablespoon butter. When the butter melts, spoon the batter onto the griddle or pan, using a tablespoon to make bite-sized cocktail cakes or a scant ¼ cup (2 fl oz/60 ml) to make larger cakes for a first course. Flatten the cakes with the back of a spoon so they will cook evenly. Cook, flipping once, until nicely browned and very crisp on both sides, 3–4 minutes on each side for little cakes, and 5–7 minutes on each side for larger ones. Do not let the pan get too hot, or the cakes will cook too quickly. The inside should remain a bit moist, like polenta. Transfer to a platter and place in the oven to keep warm. Repeat with the remaining batter, adding more butter as needed to prevent sticking.

5. Johnnycakes are wonderful served plain, but you may dress them up as described in the note. If serving the cakes with cocktails, arrange them on a large platter for passing. If serving as a first course, divide among individual plates. Serve immediately.

SERVES 8–10 AS AN HORS D'OEUVRE, OR 6 AS A FIRST COURSE

NUTRITIONAL ANALYSIS PER SERVING
Calories 144 (Kilojoules 605); Protein 5 g; Carbohydrates 20 g; Total Fat 5 g; Saturated Fat 3 g; Cholesterol 17 mg; Sodium 520 mg; Dietary Fiber 1 g

Lobster Salad with Cucumber and Dill

1 lb (500 g) fresh-cooked lobster meat (from about 5 lb/2.5 kg lobster in the shell), picked over for shell fragments and cut into bite-sized chunks

1 cucumber, peeled, seeded, and diced

2½ tablespoons fresh lemon juice

1 teaspoon grated lemon zest

1 small shallot, minced

salt and freshly ground pepper to taste

⅓ cup (3 fl oz/80 ml) extra-virgin olive oil

2 tablespoons minced fresh dill

4 cups (4 oz/125 g) loosely packed watercress sprigs, tough stems removed

Lobster fishing defines the very soul of Maine, whose rock-bound shoreline is shrouded in dense fog and salty seaside air. Although lobster is available year-round, it's most plentiful in the summer. Serve this elegant seasonal salad with toasted brioche slices and a chilled Chardonnay.

1. In a bowl, combine the lobster and cucumber. Set aside.

2. In a small bowl, whisk together the lemon juice, lemon zest, shallot, salt, and pepper. Whisk in the olive oil. Stir in the dill, then taste and adjust the seasonings. It should be quite zesty.

3. Pour the dressing over the lobster and toss to coat evenly. Cover the salad and refrigerate to chill and marinate for at least 30 minutes or as long as several hours.

4. Divide the watercress sprigs among chilled salad plates. Top evenly with the lobster salad and serve at once.

SERVES 4

NUTRITIONAL ANALYSIS PER SERVING
Calories 284 (Kilojoules 1,193); Protein 24 g; Carbohydrates 5 g; Total Fat 19 g;
Saturated Fat 3 g; Cholesterol 82 mg; Sodium 447 mg; Dietary Fiber 1 g

Steamer Clams with Broth and Drawn Butter

4 lb (2 kg) steamer clams, well
   scrubbed

1 cup (8 oz/250 g) butter, melted
   and kept warm

This recipe comes from the best steamer cook I know, a denizen of coastal Massachusetts who scorns the addition of any ingredient that would adulterate the natural, sweet flavor of the clams. Melted butter, of course, is acceptable. You can use salted or unsalted, whichever you prefer.

1. Before steaming the clams, ready the table: Have enough warm soup mugs and small ramekins to serve a mug of clam broth and a ramekin of melted butter per person. Also, set out a large bowl to collect the empty shells.

2. Pour water to a depth of ½ inch (12 mm) into a pot large enough to accommodate the clams and not be more than two-thirds full. (If you have a large pot outfitted with a steamer basket, use it.) Discard any clams that are gaping and do not close when tapped. Put the clams in the pot, cover with a tight-fitting lid, and place over high heat. Cook, shaking the pot once or twice to distribute the heat evenly, until all the clams have opened, 8–10 minutes from the time steam appears.

3. Using a large spoon, scoop the clams into large soup bowls, dividing them evenly and discarding any that failed to open. Pour the broth through a fine-mesh sieve into the mugs, trying to leave any grit behind in the bottom of the pot. Distribute the melted butter evenly among the ramekins at each place setting. Serve the clams immediately while they are piping hot. The best way to eat them is to pry open each shell with your fingers and pull the clam from it. Remove the membrane from the dark-colored "neck," or "foot." Dip the clam first in broth to rinse off any remaining sand, then in butter, and then pop it into your mouth. Some people like to sip the clam broth. Be careful, as there is always some sand at the bottom of the mug.

SERVES 4–6

NUTRITIONAL ANALYSIS PER SERVING
Calories 366 (Kilojoules 1,537); Protein 7 g; Carbohydrates 1 g; Total Fat 37 g;
Saturated Fat 23 g; Cholesterol 118 mg; Sodium 406 mg; Dietary Fiber 0 g

The bounty of clams found in shallow tidal waters of the North Atlantic is one of New England's greatest natural resources. Two main types of clams exist here, hard-shell clams, known as quahogs, and soft-shell clams, referred to as steamer, long-neck, or pisser clams.

Quahogs (pronounced "coe-hogs"), which are round and have tightly closed shells, are categorized by size. The smaller and younger the clam, the more tender the meat. The largest quahogs (chowder clams) are most often used in chowders, pies, and stuffings. Smaller hard-shell clams, called littlenecks and cherrystones, are eaten raw or steamed or used in pasta sauces and soups.

Steamer clams have a brittle, elongated shell with a protruding black "neck," or "foot." Although steamers, as their name suggests, are typically steamed and served with clam broth and butter, they are also breaded and deep-fried. Connoisseurs of fried clams will tell you that only clam bellies, or whole clams, are worth eating. Clam strips, from which the bellies have been removed, are a distant second.

Clams **Clams** Clams

While plenty of locals still dig for clams at low tide, many more folks choose to wait in line at the casual, friendly eateries, affectionately referred to as clamshacks, that operate up and down the coast. Two classic examples, the Clam Box, in Ipswich, Massachusetts, and Wood-man's, in nearby Essex, promise generous plates of fried fresh clams.

New England Clam Chowder

4 lb (2 kg) clams, preferably little-necks or Maine mahogany, well scrubbed

½ cup (4 fl oz/125 ml) water

3 slices thick-cut bacon, cut into ½-inch (12-mm) pieces

1 tablespoon unsalted butter

1 large yellow onion, chopped

2 small inner celery stalks with leaves, chopped

½ teaspoon fresh thyme, or pinch of dried

¾ lb (375 g) red or white boiling potatoes, peeled and cut into ½-inch (12-mm) dice

2 cups (16 fl oz/500 ml) half-and-half (half cream)

1½–2 cups (12–16 fl oz/375–500 ml) milk, or as needed

freshly ground pepper to taste

From Massachusetts north, clam chowder is always creamy and white. It is only from Rhode Island south that cooks dare to introduce tomatoes to the pot. Serve the chowder with soda crackers, common crackers, or crusty bread.

1. Discard any clams that are gaping and do not close when tapped. Put the clams and water in a large pot, cover with a tight-fitting lid, and place over high heat. Cook, shaking the pot once or twice to distribute the heat evenly, until the clams have opened, about 4 minutes.

2. Using a slotted spoon, scoop the clams into a bowl to cool, leaving the broth behind. Discard any clams that failed to open. Strain the broth through a double layer of cheesecloth (muslin) to eliminate any sand. Measure and add enough water to make 2 cups (16 fl oz/500 ml). Set aside.

3. In a heavy soup pot over medium heat, fry the bacon until crisp, about 5 minutes. Using a slotted spoon, transfer the bacon to paper towels to drain. Add the butter to the bacon drippings remaining in the pot over medium heat. Stir in the onion, celery, and thyme and cook until the onion is translucent, about 10 minutes. Do not allow to brown. Add the potatoes and the reserved broth and simmer, uncovered, until the potatoes are almost tender, 10–12 minutes.

4. While the potatoes are cooking, remove the clams from their shells, discarding the shells and being careful to capture their juices in the bowl. Add the clams and juices to the soup. Stir in the half-and-half and enough milk to arrive at a nice consistency that appeals to you. Bring to just below a simmer and heat to serving temperature. Do not allow to boil.

5. Add the bacon and season with pepper (it should be plenty salty from the clams). Ladle into warmed bowls and serve at once.

SERVES 8 AS A FIRST COURSE, OR 5 AS A MAIN COURSE

NUTRITIONAL ANALYSIS PER SERVING
Calories 271 (Kilojoules 1,138); Protein 10 g; Carbohydrates 16 g; Total Fat 19 g; Saturated Fat 9 g; Cholesterol 55 mg; Sodium 178 mg; Dietary Fiber 1 g

Baked Stuffed Mussels

2 slices bacon

2 lb (1 kg) mussels, well scrubbed and debearded

½ cup (4 fl oz/125 ml) dry vermouth, dry white wine, or water

rock salt as needed (optional)

¼ cup (2 oz/60 g) unsalted butter, at room temperature

¼ cup (⅓ oz/10 g) chopped fresh flat-leaf (Italian) parsley

2 tablespoons chopped fresh tarragon

1 shallot, minced

1½ teaspoons fresh lemon juice

¼ teaspoon grated lemon zest

¼ teaspoon salt

Mussel farming is big business off the crenulated coast of Maine, especially in beautiful Long Cove, where Great Eastern Mussel Farms harvests as many as 3,500 bushels (122,500 l) a week. Nestle the baked mussels in a bed of rock salt or seaweed on individual plates as a starter, or on a platter to pass at a cocktail party.

1. In a frying pan over medium heat, fry the bacon slices until crisp, about 8 minutes. Using tongs or a fork, transfer to paper towels to drain. Chop finely and set aside.

2. Discard any mussels that are gaping and do not close when tapped. In a wide saucepan, combine the mussels and the vermouth, white wine, or water. Cover with a tight-fitting lid and place over high heat. Cook, shaking the pan once or twice to distribute the heat evenly, until the mussels begin to open, about 4 minutes. Drain the mussels and set aside to cool. Discard any mussels that failed to open.

3. Preheat the oven to 350°F (180°C). Make a bed of rock salt or crumpled aluminum foil on a baking sheet. The bed should be deep enough to steady the mussels once they are stuffed.

4. In a small bowl, combine the chopped bacon, butter, parsley, tarragon, shallot, lemon juice, lemon zest, and salt. Using a wooden spoon, work the ingredients together until evenly mixed. Set aside.

5. Remove the mussels from their shells, discarding one shell from each and nestling the remaining shell on the prepared baking sheet. If any of the tough, wiry "beard" remains on a mussel, trim it off. Place 1 mussel in each shell. Spoon a small dollop of the butter mixture on top, using ¼–½ teaspoon for each mussel, depending on its size. Bake until the butter begins to bubble, about 10 minutes. Serve immediately.

SERVES 6

NUTRITIONAL ANALYSIS PER SERVING
Calories 123 (Kilojoules 517); Protein 6 g; Carbohydrates 3 g; Total Fat 10 g; Saturated Fat 5 g; Cholesterol 35 mg; Sodium 257 mg; Dietary Fiber 0 g

Pilgrims'
Progress

A driving tour through New England's countryside reveals a bucolic landscape dotted with white clapboard churches, tidy town greens, winding country roads, and fertile pasturelands bordered by low stone walls. The picture-postcard scenes, however, belie a landscape that has been dramatically transformed over the centuries.

Before the colonies were settled, the Northeast was covered with an almost unbroken forest. Once the white settlers arrived, they cut the trees to create farmland and to provide lumber and potash to the growing cities. This lasted for about two hundred years, until all but 20 percent of the region's original forests were destroyed. Then, when canals, turnpikes, and railways began to link New England with the fertile farmlands and expansive forests of the West and Midwest, the trend reversed. New England's depleted forest and patchwork of small farms were no match for the vast resources found beyond the Ohio River Valley. Many farmers and loggers abandoned their holdings, and the region's agrarian economy collapsed. Over the century, the forestlands regenerated and farming continued to dwindle until, by 1960, 80 percent of the region was reforested and 85 percent of New England's food came from elsewhere.

Around this same time, a reverse migration of people occurred, with folks leaving the more-developed urban areas for the less-crowded reaches of New England. Many of these urban transplants bought and restored old farms and took up small-scale farming as a means of getting back to the land.

In 1971, a group of these idealistic, new-generation homesteaders and farmers from New Hampshire and Vermont gathered to talk about rev-olutionizing the modern-day food system by growing organic food and selling it locally. Their unofficial leader was Samuel Kaymen, a rugged indi-vidualist who is one of the country's foremost authorities on organic and biodynamic agriculture and a cofounder of Stoneyfield Farm in Londonderry, New Hampshire. Together this visionary bunch of farmers and gardeners dreamed up the Northeast Organic Farmers Association (NOFA). The first organ-ization of its kind in the United States, it has grown to become one of the nation's largest organic associations.

At first, the local organic pro-duce, meats, and other products were available only at farmers' mar-kets, farm stands, and health-food stores. Now, thanks to the efforts of regional chefs and growers, and to the public's increased appetite for wholesome foods, these health-ful ingredients also appear season-ally in mainstream restaurants and supermarkets throughout the region.

Organic fruits and vegetables such as greens, heirloom toma-toes, and squashes (opposite), as well as packaged organic products (below), are now widely available in New England.

Winter Squash Soup with Sage Cream

12 fresh sage leaves with stems intact, coarsely chopped

½ cup (4 fl oz/125 ml) heavy (double) cream

pinch of salt

pinch of freshly ground pepper

2 tablespoons unsalted butter

2 yellow onions, chopped

1 celery stalk, chopped

2½–3 lb (1.25–1.5 kg) winter squash, peeled, seeded, and cut into 1-inch (2.5-cm) chunks

2 cloves garlic, minced

¾ teaspoon salt, plus salt to taste

¼ teaspoon freshly ground pepper, plus pepper to taste

4 cups (32 fl oz/1 l) chicken or vegetable stock or water

A colorful display of winter squashes announces the arrival of fall each year at New England's local farmers' markets. Choose from butternut, acorn, kabocha, or Hubbard squash for this golden soup that makes a warming first course or a light supper when accompanied with crusty bread.

1. To make the sage cream, combine the sage and cream in a small saucepan. Place over medium heat and heat until small bubbles appear along the edges of the pan. Remove from the heat, cover, and let stand for 20 minutes.

2. Strain the sage-infused cream through a fine-mesh sieve into a small bowl. Season with the salt and pepper, cover, and chill well.

3. To make the soup, melt the butter in a wide soup pot over medium heat. Add the onions and celery and cook, stirring often, until very soft, 8–10 minutes; do not allow to brown. Stir in the squash chunks, garlic, the ¾ teaspoon salt, and the ¼ teaspoon pepper, and cook, stirring, for 1 minute longer. Add the stock or water and bring to a simmer. Cover partially and cook until the squash is soft enough to mash against the side of the pot, 20–25 minutes. Remove from the heat.

4. In a blender or food processor, purée the soup in batches and transfer to a clean saucepan. Reheat gently over medium heat and season with salt and pepper. While the soup is reheating, quickly whisk the sage cream to make it a bit frothy.

5. Ladle the soup into warmed bowls and top each serving with a swirl of the sage cream. Serve immediately.

SERVES 6 AS A FIRST COURSE, OR 4 AS A MAIN COURSE

NUTRITIONAL ANALYSIS PER SERVING
Calories 202 (Kilojoules 848); Protein 5 g; Carbohydrates 20 g; Total Fat 13 g; Saturated Fat 7 g; Cholesterol 38 mg; Sodium 1,002 mg; Dietary Fiber 4 g

White Pizza with Sardines

DOUGH

1 teaspoon active dry yeast

¾ cup (6 fl oz/180 ml) lukewarm
water (105°F/40°C)

1½–2 cups (7½–10 oz/235–315 g)
all-purpose (plain) flour

1½ teaspoons coarse salt

1 tablespoon extra-virgin olive oil

TOPPING

2 tablespoons extra-virgin olive oil

2 or 3 cloves garlic, minced

1 tablespoon chopped fresh oregano,
or 1 teaspoon dried

1 teaspoon grated lemon zest

½ red (Spanish) onion, sliced into
thin rings

1 tin (3¾ oz/110 g) sardines, drained
and cut into 1-inch (2.5-cm) pieces

⅓ cup (1½ oz/45 g) grated
Parmesan cheese

2 tablespoons chopped fresh flat-leaf
(Italian) parsley

freshly ground pepper to taste

This version of *pizza bianca* honors the busy sardine canneries that once proliferated along the Maine coast.

1. To make the dough, in a large bowl, sprinkle the yeast over the lukewarm water. Using a wooden spoon, stir in 1½ cups (7½ oz/235 g) of the flour, the coarse salt, and the olive oil. When the dough becomes too stiff to stir, transfer it to a floured work surface and knead until smooth and elastic, 6–10 minutes, adding up to ½ cup (2½ oz/80 g) more flour as needed to reduce the stickiness. (Alternatively, use a stand mixer, stirring with a spoon as directed, then kneading on low speed with a dough hook.) Form the dough into a ball and place in an oiled bowl. Turn the ball to coat on all sides with the oil, then cover the bowl with plastic wrap and let stand in a warm place until the dough is doubled in size, 2–2½ hours.

2. Meanwhile, begin making the topping: In a small bowl, stir together the oil, garlic, oregano, and lemon zest. Let stand for 2 hours.

3. If you have a pizza stone, put it on the bottom rack in the oven. Preheat the oven to 475°F (245°C). Allow the pizza stone to heat for at least 45 minutes before baking.

4. Punch down the dough in the bowl and let it rest for 30 minutes. Then turn it out onto a well-floured work surface and roll it out into a round 12–14 inches (30–35 cm) in diameter and about ¼ inch (6 mm) thick. Do not make a lip on the pizza. Let it rest for 15 minutes.

5. Transfer the round to a baker's peel or rimless baking sheet if using a pizza stone, or to a baking sheet if not using a stone. Brush the olive oil mixture over the dough. Scatter the onion rings and sardine pieces evenly on top, then sprinkle with the cheese. Slide the pizza onto the stone, if using, or place the baking sheet on the bottom rack in the oven. Bake the pizza until the bottom of the crust is brown, about 12 minutes. Remove from the oven and top with the parsley and pepper. Serve hot.

SERVES 8

NUTRITIONAL ANALYSIS PER SERVING
Calories 226 (Kilojoules 949); Protein 9 g; Carbohydrates 27 g; Total Fat 9 g;
Saturated Fat 2 g; Cholesterol 21 mg; Sodium 436 mg; Dietary Fiber 1 g

Shaker Herb Salad

1 cup (1 oz/30 g) loosely packed fresh flat-leaf (Italian) parsley leaves

1 cup (1 oz/30 g) loosely packed arugula (rocket) leaves

1 cup (1 oz/30 g) loosely packed fresh basil leaves

¾ cup (¾ oz/20 g) fresh chervil sprigs

¾ cup (¾ oz/20 g) loosely packed sorrel or baby spinach leaves

⅓ cup (½ oz/15 g) chopped fresh chives

⅓ cup (⅓ oz/10 g) fresh tarragon leaves

salt and freshly ground pepper to taste

3 tablespoons extra-virgin olive oil, or to taste

2–3 teaspoons fresh lemon juice

The Shakers of New England were great herbalists, gathering and cultivating herbs for medicine as well as for the kitchen. Serve this zesty salad in small portions alongside rich meats and fish, or mound a bit of it in the center of a few slices of prosciutto or salami for a light lunch or starter.

1. Carefully pick over all of the herbs and tear any larger leaves into bite-sized pieces. Wash and dry gently, but thoroughly, in a salad spinner or a kitchen towel. The more delicate leaves such as basil and tarragon will bruise if handled roughly. Combine all the greens in a salad bowl. (The salad may be prepared up to this point, covered with a damp kitchen towel, and refrigerated for several hours.)

2. Season the greens with salt and pepper. Drizzle on the olive oil and toss to coat all the greens lightly. Add the lemon juice to taste and toss again. Serve immediately.

SERVES 4–6

NUTRITIONAL ANALYSIS PER SERVING
Calories 86 (Kilojoules 361); Protein 1 g; Carbohydrates 2 g; Total Fat 9 g; Saturated Fat 1 g; Cholesterol 0 mg; Sodium 6 mg; Dietary Fiber 1 g

All that remains of the once-thriving Shaker communities of the Northeast are a few villages and museums, yet this industrious and idealistic religious sect made a lasting contribution to the foods of the region. In their heyday in the mid-1800s, some six thousand Shakers, so-called for their rapturous trembling during worship, were living in nineteen rural communities throughout Massachusetts, Maine, and New Hampshire.

Committed to the principles of simplicity and industry, the Shakers won a well-deserved reputation as craftspeople, accomplished cooks, and innovative gardeners. Part of their influence came from the cottage industries they set up to earn them enough income to support their communities. The Shakers cultivated medicinal and culinary herbs for sale, were the first to package seeds to sell to other gardeners, and were well known for their top-quality fruit preserves, which were readily sold "by the bottle and by the gallon."

Although the ideals of the Shaker movement are some two hundred years old, they are remarkably similar to the sentiments of today's best cooks. The Shakers recognized that

The **Shaker** Tradition

good food was the basis of a good life, and they believed in cooking only with natural ingredients. A few Shaker cookbooks still exist, and the appealing recipes—Poached Salmon with Minted Sweet Pea Cream, Roast Lamb with Ginger and Cider, Honey Lavender Ice Cream—indicate that Shaker food would taste as good to us today as it must have then.

French-Canadian Pea Soup with Salt Herbs

2 rounded cups (1 lb/500 kg) dried yellow split peas

2 small smoked or fresh ham hocks, about 1 lb (500 g) total

1 large yellow onion, chopped

1 carrot, peeled and finely chopped

1 bay leaf

2 teaspoons coarse salt, plus salt to taste

8 cups (64 fl oz/2 l) water

1 cup (2 oz/60 g) packed spinach leaves without stems

3 tablespoons chopped fresh chives

2 tablespoons chopped fresh marjoram or oregano

freshly ground pepper to taste

In the robust French-Canadian communities across the northern borderlands of New England, cooks preserve fresh summer herbs and greens with salt. Here, a shortcut version of the traditional recipe is used to add a bit of color and zest to a smooth and light split pea soup.

1. Pick over the split peas, discarding any stones or misshapen peas. Rinse well and place in a soup pot with the ham hocks, onion, carrot, bay leaf, 1 teaspoon of the salt, and the water. Bring to a boil over high heat. Skim off any foam from the surface, reduce the heat to medium, cover partially, and simmer until the peas are falling apart and the meat on the ham hocks is fork tender, about 1 hour.

2. Meanwhile, in a small food processor, combine the spinach, chives, marjoram or oregano, and the remaining 1 teaspoon salt. Pulse, scraping down the sides of the work bowl occasionally, until a paste of sorts forms. Alternatively, pile the spinach, chives, and marjoram or oregano on a clean cutting board. Sprinkle on the remaining 1 teaspoon salt and chop the herbs with a large chef's knife until you achieve a pastelike consistency. Transfer the paste to a small dish and set aside.

3. Remove the ham hocks from the pot and set aside. Remove and discard the bay leaf. Using a blender or a food processor, purée the soup in batches and return it to a clean saucepan. When the ham is cool enough to handle, remove it from the bones, discarding the skin, fat, and bones. Cut the meat into a small dice and add it to the soup.

4. Bring the soup to a simmer over medium-low heat and season with pepper. Ladle into warmed bowls and add a teaspoonful of the salt herbs to each bowl. Serve immediately.

SERVES 8 AS A FIRST COURSE, OR 5 AS A MAIN COURSE

NUTRITIONAL ANALYSIS PER SERVING
Calories 239 (Kilojoules 1,004); Protein 19 g; Carbohydrates 38 g; Total Fat 2 g; Saturated Fat 0 g; Cholesterol 10 mg; Sodium 691 mg; Dietary Fiber 4 g

Salt Cod and Potato Cakes

1 lb (500 g) boneless, skinless salt cod

3 cups (24 fl oz/750 ml) milk, or
 as needed

1 lb (500 g) russet potatoes, peeled
 and diced

3 tablespoons unsalted butter

4 green (spring) onions, white and
 pale green parts only, finely
 chopped

2 cloves garlic, minced

2 eggs, lightly beaten

½ teaspoon salt

freshly ground pepper to taste

1 cup (2 oz/60 g) fresh bread crumbs

½ cup (2 oz/60 g) grated Parmesan
 cheese

2 tablespoons olive oil, or as needed

1 lemon, cut into wedges (optional)

Fish cakes have long been a staple in New England's cod-fishing communities, where they are often fried up in bacon fat for breakfast. This more uptown version makes an excellent starter accompanied with tomato salsa.

1. Place the salt cod in a bowl, add cold water to cover, and refrigerate for 12–18 hours, changing the water 3 or 4 times.

2. Drain the cod and place in a saucepan. Add enough milk to the pan to cover the cod, and place the pan over medium heat. Bring to a simmer and cook gently until tender, 15–20 minutes. Drain and, when cool enough to handle, remove any errant bits of skin or bones. Place the fish in a large bowl and, using a fork, flake it into small bits.

3. Meanwhile, place the potatoes in a saucepan and add water to cover. Bring to a boil over high heat, reduce the heat to medium, and simmer, uncovered, until tender, 10–15 minutes. Drain and pass through a ricer placed over a bowl, or mash with a potato masher until smooth. Stir in 2 tablespoons of the butter until melted. Then stir the potatoes into the cod along with the green onions, garlic, eggs, salt, and pepper.

4. Preheat the oven to 200°F (95°C). In a shallow plate, stir together the bread crumbs and cheese. Shape the cod-potato mixture into patties each 3 inches (7.5 cm) in diameter and ¾ inch (2 cm) thick. Coat the patties on both sides with the crumb mixture.

5. In a large frying pan over medium heat, warm 2 tablespoons olive oil and the remaining 1 tablespoon butter. In batches, add the cakes and fry, turning once, until browned and heated through, 2–4 minutes on each side. Transfer to the oven to keep warm. Cook the remaining cakes, adding more oil if necessary.

6. Serve the cakes on warmed plates with lemon wedges, if desired.

MAKES ABOUT TWELVE 3-INCH (7.5-CM) CAKES; SERVES 6–8

NUTRITIONAL ANALYSIS PER SERVING
Calories 400 (Kilojoules 1,680); Protein 48 g; Carbohydrates 16 g; Total Fat 15 g;
Saturated Fat 6 g; Cholesterol 180 mg; Sodium *n/a*; Dietary Fiber 1 g

Mushroom, Chicken, and Barley Soup

This comforting soup is inspired by Scotch broth, a hearty lamb and barley soup made by the many cooks of Scottish descent residing in New England. Serve it in the fall and early spring when woodland mushrooms are at their best.

1. Rinse the barley under cold water, place in a bowl, and add water to cover. Let soak for 2–3 hours.

2. Rinse the chicken pieces well and place in a large pot. Add the stock or water to cover. Bring to a simmer over medium heat, cover partially, and simmer gently, skimming occasionally, until cooked through and the juices run clear when the thickest part of a thigh is pricked with a knife, about 15 minutes. Using a slotted spoon, transfer the chicken to a dish and set aside to cool. Reserve the stock.

3. In a wide soup pot over high heat, warm the olive oil. Add the mushrooms, season with salt and pepper, and cook, stirring often, until the mushrooms begin to brown and shrink, 5–7 minutes. (If necessary, cook the mushrooms in two batches; they should not be more than a single layer deep.) Add the leek, shallot, and 2 tablespoons parsley and cook, stirring, for 1 minute longer. Stir in the sherry or Madeira and bring the mixture to a boil.

4. Drain the barley and add it to the pot along with the reserved stock. Bring to a boil, then reduce the heat to medium-low. Cover partially and simmer gently until the barley is tender, about 20 minutes.

5. Meanwhile, discard the skin and bones from the chicken pieces and cut the meat into bite-sized pieces. Add the chicken to the soup and heat through. Taste and adjust the seasonings.

6. Ladle into warmed bowls and garnish with parsley. Serve immediately.

SERVES 6 AS A FIRST COURSE, OR 4 AS A MAIN COURSE

NUTRITIONAL ANALYSIS PER SERVING
Calories 361 (Kilojoules 1,516); Protein 32 g; Carbohydrates 22 g; Total Fat 15 g; Saturated Fat 3 g; Cholesterol 93 mg; Sodium 775 mg; Dietary Fiber 4 g

½ cup (4 oz/125 g) pearl barley

1 chicken, about 3½ lb (1.75 kg), cut into serving pieces and trimmed of excess fat

4 cups (32 fl oz/1 l) chicken stock or water, or as needed

2 tablespoons olive oil

1 lb (500 g) assorted fresh wild or cultivated mushrooms, brushed clean, tough stems removed, and thickly sliced

salt and freshly ground pepper to taste

1 leek, white part only, chopped

1 shallot, minced

2 tablespoons chopped fresh flat-leaf (Italian) parsley, plus extra for garnish

¼ cup (2 fl oz/60 ml) dry sherry or Madeira wine

Vermont Cheddar and Walnut Crisps

1½ cups (7½ oz/235 g) all-purpose (plain) flour

½ cup (2 oz/60 g) finely chopped walnuts

½ teaspoon freshly ground pepper

½ teaspoon salt

½ cup (4 oz/125 g) chilled unsalted butter, cut into ¼-inch (6-mm) pieces

1¼ cups (5 oz/155 g) shredded sharp cheddar cheese

1 egg yolk

2 tablespoons cream or milk

A perfect snack to serve with cocktails, these savory wafers highlight the much-acclaimed aged cheddar cheeses made in Vermont. A mix of cheddar and Parmesan will work, too.

1. In a food processor, combine the flour, nuts, pepper, and salt. Process briefly to mix. Drop in the butter and pulse until the butter forms pea-sized pieces. Add the cheddar cheese and process until well mixed. Finally, drop in the egg yolk, add the cream or milk, and pulse only until the dough comes together. Alternatively, in a large bowl, stir together the flour, nuts, pepper, and salt. Add the butter and, using a pastry blender or 2 table knives, cut in the butter until it forms pea-sized pieces. Using a rubber spatula, quickly stir in the cheese. Finally, add the egg yolk and cream or milk and work these quickly into the dough using the rubber spatula. Turn the dough out onto a floured work surface and shape it into a thick, flat disk. Wrap in plastic wrap and refrigerate for at least 1 hour.

2. Preheat the oven to 400°F (200°C).

3. Sprinkle the work surface lightly with flour, then roll out the dough about ¼ inch (6 mm) thick. If it begins to crumble, press any fissures together with your fingers. Using a cookie cutter or a knife, cut out shapes of any sort about 1½ inches (4 cm) across. Arrange them on 2 ungreased baking sheets, spacing them about ½ inch (12 mm) apart. Gather up the scraps, reroll, cut out more shapes, and add to the baking sheets.

4. Bake until lightly browned, about 14 minutes, switching the baking sheets halfway through so the crisps cook evenly. To test, break a crisp in half to see if the inside is cooked. If not, bake for another few minutes. Transfer to a rack to cool.

5. Serve the crisps within a few hours or store in an airtight container at room temperature for up to a few days.

MAKES ABOUT 6 DOZEN CRISPS

NUTRITIONAL ANALYSIS PER CRISP
Calories 38 (Kilojoules 160); Protein 1 g; Carbohydrates 3 g; Total Fat 3 g;
Saturated Fat 1 g; Cholesterol 9 mg; Sodium 29 mg; Dietary Fiber 0 g

The cheese most closely associated with New England is cheddar. Early settlers brought cheddaring techniques from England and began making the familiar sharp, firm cheese as a way to preserve milk. American-made cheddar was referred to as Yankee cheese, rat cheese, or store cheese and was sold from large blocks in every general store, a practice that continues in many towns today.

By the mid-nineteenth century, cheese makers in the United States developed the means to manufacture their products on a large scale. Fortunately, factory cheese making never completely took over, and a few original producers of distinctive handmade cheddar cheese are still in business today, such as Crowley Cheese Company and Grafton Village Cheese, both in Vermont.

In recent years, these traditional companies have been joined by leagues of cheese artisans, and the range of quality cheese made in the region has increased tremendously. For example, at the 1999 annual conference of the American Cheese Society, an organization dedicated to perpetuating superior farmstead cheese nationally, New England took

Farmstead **Cheeses**

close to 40 percent of the first-place ribbons for such products as Lazy Lady's soft-ripened goat cheese from Vermont; queso blanco from Calabro Cheese Company in Connecticut; a blue-veined goat cheese from Westfield Farm in Massachusetts; and, with a bow to tradition, Shelburne Farms's famous farmhouse Vermont cheddar.

Cabbage Salad with Pears and Goat Cheese

1 teaspoon cumin seeds or ¼ teaspoon ground cumin

1 small head green cabbage, about
1¾ lb (875 g)

3 tablespoons olive oil

1 teaspoon coarse salt

1 teaspoon sugar

¼ cup (2 fl oz/60 ml) white wine
vinegar

2 pears, preferably Anjou or Bosc,
peeled, quartered, cored, and
thinly sliced lengthwise

¼ lb (4 oz/125 g) fresh goat cheese,
crumbled

2 tablespoons chopped fresh parsley
or chives

freshly ground pepper to taste

This refreshing winter salad highlights the exceptional fresh goat cheeses that are now made on small farms all over New England. Serve it as a salad course, as an accompaniment to roast pork or chicken, or tossed with pasta as a vegetarian main course.

1. If using cumin seeds, in a small, dry frying pan over medium-low heat, toast the cumin seeds, shaking the pan to toast evenly, until they take on a little color and are fragrant, about 2 minutes. Remove from the heat, place in a mortar, and crush lightly. Set aside. If using ground cumin, reserve.

2. Remove the outer leaves from the cabbage and discard. Cut the cabbage into quarters through the stem end, cut away the tough core, and then thinly slice the quarters crosswise. Ready all the ingredients and place alongside the stove before you begin to cook.

3. In a large frying pan over high heat, warm the olive oil. Add the cabbage and sauté, tossing often, until evenly coated with oil, about 1 minute. Add the salt, sugar, cumin, and vinegar, then cover and continue to cook until the cabbage is heated through and begins to soften, 2–4 minutes. Uncover and add the pear slices. Cook uncovered, stirring once or twice, for 1 minute longer.

4. Remove the pan from the heat and transfer the contents to a large serving bowl. Add the goat cheese, parsley or chives, and a few grinds of pepper. Toss to combine, then taste and adjust the seasonings.

5. Serve warm or at room temperature.

SERVES 6

NUTRITIONAL ANALYSIS PER SERVING
Calories 174 (Kilojoules 731); Protein 5 g; Carbohydrates 15 g; Total Fat 11 g; Saturated Fat 4 g; Cholesterol 9 mg; Sodium 335 mg; Dietary Fiber 4 g

BAKED BEAN
SUPPER
at
TOPSHAM
GRANGE HALL

TO BENEFIT
TOPSHAM E.M.S.
ASSOC.

This Saturday   Sat. 5-6:30 PM

WATCH
FOR
TURNING
TRAFFIC

2 Seafood, Poultry & Meats

Whether it's an herb-studded pork roast, broiled bluefish, or a mix of sausages and clams, the main course is considered by New England cooks to be the most important and, quite often, the only part of a meal. This is due in no small measure to the fact that the region boasts such a wonderful variety of local seafood, poultry, and meat—ingredients that easily merit the full attention of the cook and the diners. The recipes that follow reflect the taste for the simple, hearty meals that New Englanders have long favored.

Broiled Bluefish with Tomato-Basil Relish

RELISH

½ pt (8 oz/250 g) currant or other
small cherry tomatoes, a mixture
of red and yellow if possible,
stems removed

2 or 3 green (spring) onions, white
and pale green parts only, finely
chopped (¼ cup/¾ oz/20 g)

⅓–½ cup (⅓–½ oz/10–15 g) loosely
packed fresh basil leaves, cut into
narrow strips

2 tablespoons extra-virgin olive oil

1 tablespoon capers, roughly chopped

1 small clove garlic, crushed and
minced

1 teaspoon sherry vinegar or red
wine vinegar

salt and freshly ground pepper
to taste

olive oil for brushing

2 small or 1 large bluefish fillet,
preferably with skin on, 1½–2 lb
(750 g–1 kg) total weight

1 teaspoon chopped fresh thyme, or
½ teaspoon dried thyme

salt and freshly ground pepper
to taste

Large schools of beautiful, spirited bluefish migrate to New England's shallow coastal waters every summer. The zesty tomato-basil relish that accompanies the bluefish here is also good with tuna, salmon, or swordfish steaks. Serve the fish with boiled new potatoes, a rice pilaf, or bread.

1. To make the relish, halve the tomatoes, or quarter them if larger than a gumball. Put them in a bowl with the green onions, basil, olive oil, capers, garlic, and vinegar. Toss lightly to combine, then season with salt and pepper. (The relish may be made several hours ahead, but do not refrigerate.)

2. Preheat the broiler (griller). Cover the broiler pan with aluminum foil and brush the foil with olive oil.

3. Arrange the fillet(s), skin side down, on the foil and brush the top(s) with more olive oil. Sprinkle the fillet(s) with the thyme, salt, and pepper.

4. Position the broiler pan so that the top of the fish is about 4 inches (10 cm) below the heat source and broil (grill) the fillet(s) for 3–4 minutes if they are less than 1 inch (2.5 cm) thick, or 5–7 minutes for thicker fillet(s). Flip carefully and broil for another 4 minutes for thinner fillet(s), or 6 minutes for thicker fillet(s).

5. Transfer the fish to a warmed platter and divide into 4 serving pieces. Spoon the tomato relish over the top and serve at once.

SERVES 4

NUTRITIONAL ANALYSIS PER SERVING
Calories 311 (Kilojoules 1,306); Protein 38 g; Carbohydrates 4 g; Total Fat 15 g;
Saturated Fat 3 g; Cholesterol 110 mg; Sodium 214 mg; Dietary Fiber 1 g

New England
Fisheries

From the earliest days, Native Americans referred to the region around Massachusetts as Naumkeag, meaning "fishing place," and indeed the first European settlers marveled at the abundance and diversity of fish and shellfish in the coastal waters. With the establishment of fishing communities like Gloucester and New Bedford in the seventeenth century, the sea became the focus of life in New England.

From the start, the fishing industry was centered on groundfish, including Atlantic cod, haddock, redfish, hake, pollock, and flounder. So named for their tendency to swim near the bottom of the sea, groundfish proliferate in the North Atlantic because of a string of huge shoals where warm gulf currents meet cold Arctic waters and create a fertile marine environment. One of the richest and most productive of these shoals, known as Georges Bank, sits about a day's sail off the coast of Massachusetts and is larger than the state itself.

Besides groundfish, New England seamen also pull in the bluefish, striped bass, tuna, and swordfish that migrate up to the cooler waters of the Gulf of Maine each summer.

Other popular fish harvested from the banks and the gulf include monkfish, mackerel, whiting, and halibut.

But New Englanders have not been content to haul in only finfish. The region's reputation for shellfish is unequaled in the country. Lobsters, oysters, and true bay scallops (especially the small, sweet Cape variety from Nantucket) are the most renowned shellfish catches, but clams, sea scallops, mussels, crabs, sea urchins, and shrimp (prawns) are also harvested in the various waterways up and down the coast. Some of the finest oysters in the country, such as Wellfleets, Rhode Island Selects, Cotuits, Cedar Points, and Pemaquids, live in these icy waters. Plus, over 90 percent of the nation's lobster supply comes from Maine.

Despite the rich past and present of New England's fisheries, their future is in question. Centuries of ambitious, independent fishermen and the introduction of factory trawlers (large barges capable of processing fish at sea) in the 1940s have nearly depleted the stocks of cod, swordfish, and other species.

In recent decades, the government has imposed strict fishing regulations between Cape Cod and the tip of Maine in an attempt to protect the remaining fish and to allow stocks to regenerate. In turn, many small-scale fishermen have been forced out of business, while others have seized opportunities in alternative enterprises, such as the rapidly expanding industry of farm-raised fish and shellfish. While we may never see stocks of cod as dense as they once were, the livelihood and character of New England remains inextricably tied to the sea.

A modest selection of New England's bounty of fish and shellfish.

Roast Cod Fillets with Horseradish-Dill Sauce

1 shallot, minced

1½–2 lb (750 g–1 kg) cod fillet, divided into 4 equal pieces

salt and freshly ground pepper to taste

6 tablespoons (3 oz/90 g) chilled unsalted butter, cut into ½-inch (12-mm) pieces

¼ cup (2 fl oz/60 ml) hard apple cider, dry apple wine, or dry white wine

2 tablespoons white wine vinegar or fresh lemon juice

2 tablespoons heavy (double) cream

1 tablespoon chopped fresh dill

1 tablespoon peeled and freshly grated or drained prepared horseradish

Poached cod with a creamy horseradish sauce is a common Yankee party dish, first popularized by the Kennedy family at their summer home on Cape Cod. This adaptation uses the same flavors to create an elegant dinner main course.

1. Preheat the oven to 400°F (200°C). Butter a shallow baking dish large enough to accommodate the fillets in a single layer.

2. Sprinkle the prepared baking dish with half of the minced shallot. Rinse the fish, pat dry with paper towels, season with salt and pepper, and arrange, skin side down, on the shallot. (If the skin has been removed, you can recognize the skin side by a thin opaque membrane covering the fish.) Cut 1 piece of the butter into thin slices and use to dot the tops of the fillets. Set aside while you make the sauce.

3. In a small saucepan over high heat, combine the remaining shallot with the cider or wine and the vinegar or lemon juice. Bring to a boil, reduce the heat to medium, and cook until the liquid is almost evaporated, about 10 minutes. Add the cream and simmer for 1 minute longer. Reduce the heat to the lowest setting, then whisk in the remaining 5½ table-spoons (2½ oz/75 g) butter until smooth. (You will be pushing the butter around at first but it will gradually melt.) Don't let the sauce get too hot, or the butter will separate. Stir in the dill and horseradish and season with salt and pepper. Cover and set in a warm spot off the heat.

4. Place the fish in the oven and bake until opaque throughout, 10–13 minutes. The timing will depend upon the thickness of the fillets.

5. Using a spatula, transfer the fillets to warmed individual plates. Spoon a little of the warm sauce over each fillet and serve immediately. Pass any remaining sauce at the table.

SERVES 4

NUTRITIONAL ANALYSIS PER SERVING
Calories 355 (Kilojoules 1,491); Protein 36 g; Carbohydrates 1 g; Total Fat 21 g; Saturated Fat 13 g; Cholesterol 142 mg; Sodium 117 mg; Dietary Fiber 0 g

Shad Roe with Brown Butter and Bacon

Shad roe is a harbinger of the New England spring, and locals eagerly celebrate its arrival each year. This recipe comes from an old-timer who still cooks his shad roe on a woodstove and insists on a pair of roe per person. Smaller appetites may be satisfied with half that amount.

2 pair of shad roe, about 6 oz
  (185 g) per pair

4 slices thick-cut bacon, cut into
  ¾-inch (2-cm) pieces

¼ cup (2 oz/60 g) unsalted butter,
  cut into 4 equal pieces

salt and freshly ground pepper
  to taste

2 tablespoons fresh lemon juice

2–3 tablespoons chopped fresh parsley

1. Using a sharp paring knife, carefully separate each pair of roe. Trim off any excess membrane without cutting open the roe sac. Rinse gently under cold water, pat dry with paper towels, and set aside.

2. In a frying pan over medium heat, fry the bacon until crisp, about 5 minutes. Using a slotted spoon, transfer the bacon to paper towels to drain. Pour off all but about 2 tablespoons of the drippings from the pan.

3. Return the frying pan to the stove, reduce the heat to low, and add the butter. Once the butter has melted, season the roe with salt and pepper and slide them into the pan. Spoon some of the butter and drippings over the roe to baste them, then cover the pan and adjust the heat so that the fat is barely simmering and not burning. If you hear ferocious popping sounds, the heat is too high. Cook for 6–8 minutes, basting the tops once or twice again. Uncover the pan, gently flip the roe, re-cover the pan, and continue cooking for another 6–8 minutes. The roe is done when it is slightly firm but not hard to the touch, somewhat like a ripe plum. Overcooking will render the roe dry and bland. Using a slotted spoon, transfer the roe to warmed individual plates.

4. Raise the heat and, when the fat begins to foam, add the lemon juice. Stir briefly, then quickly remove from the heat. Add the reserved cooked bacon and the parsley to the pan and mix well. Spoon the sauce over the roe and serve immediately.

SERVES 2–4

NUTRITIONAL ANALYSIS PER SERVING
Calories 438 (Kilojoules 1,840); Protein 27 g; Carbohydrates 3 g; Total Fat 38 g; Saturated Fat 16 g; Cholesterol 481 mg; Sodium 246 mg; Dietary Fiber 0 g

Lamb Steaks with Heirloom Beans

1 cup (7 oz/220 g) dried heirloom white beans, preferably Jacob's Cattle beans

½ cup (4 fl oz/125 ml) plus 2½ tablespoons extra-virgin olive oil, plus extra for drizzling

¼ cup (2 fl oz/60 ml) fresh lemon juice, plus a few drops for seasoning

1 tablespoon chopped fresh rosemary, plus 2 sprigs

4 cloves garlic, 2 minced and 2 sliced

1 teaspoon dry mustard

2 teaspoons salt, plus salt to taste

½ teaspoon freshly ground pepper

4 lamb steaks cut from the leg, each about ½ lb (250 g) and ¾ inch (2 cm) thick

1 bay leaf

4–5 cups (32–40 fl oz/1–1.25 l) water

1 shallot, minced

2 tablespoons chopped fresh flat-leaf (Italian) parsley

Heirloom beans are available in many varieties. I prefer Jacob's Cattle beans, lovely maroon-speckled white beans from the Kennebec Bean Company of Maine. They have a moist, creamy texture and tender skin.

1. Pick over the beans and discard any stones or misshapen beans. Rinse well, place in a bowl, and add water to cover; let soak overnight.

2. In a shallow nonaluminum dish, stir together the ½ cup (4 fl oz/125 ml) olive oil, the ¼ cup (2 fl oz/60 ml) lemon juice, the chopped rosemary, the minced garlic, the dry mustard, 1 teaspoon of the salt, and the pepper. Place the lamb steaks in the marinade, turn to coat, cover, and refrigerate, turning 2 or 3 times, for 3–4 hours.

3. Drain the beans and put them in a saucepan with the sliced garlic, ½ tablespoon of the remaining oil, the rosemary sprigs, bay leaf, and water to cover by 1 inch (2.5 cm). Place over medium heat, bring to a simmer, cover partially, and simmer very gently until tender, 1–2 hours, adding the remaining 1 teaspoon salt and more water, if needed, after 45 minutes. Remove from the heat and set aside while you cook the steaks.

4. Preheat the broiler (griller) or a stove-top grill pan over high heat.

5. Wipe the excess marinade from the steaks. Position the broiler pan 3–4 inches (7.5–10 cm) below the heat source. Broil (grill) the steaks for 4–5 minutes. Flip them and cook for 4 minutes longer for medium-rare. They are best served still pink in the center.

6. Just before the lamb steaks are done, drain the beans and toss with the shallot, the remaining 2 tablespoons olive oil, and the chopped parsley. Season with a few drops of lemon juice and salt and pepper.

7. Transfer the steaks to warmed individual plates and place a spoonful of beans alongside. Drizzle olive oil over the beans, then serve.

SERVES 4

NUTRITIONAL ANALYSIS PER SERVING
Calories 618 (Kilojoules 2,596); Protein 45 g; Carbohydrates 32 g; Total Fat 35 g; Saturated Fat 11 g; Cholesterol 122 mg; Sodium 751 mg; Dietary Fiber 20 g

Quail Roasted with Concord Grapes

8 quail, about 6 oz (185 g) each

4 tablespoons olive oil

salt to taste, plus ½ teaspoon

freshly ground pepper to taste,
   plus ¼ teaspoon

2 slices pancetta or bacon, each cut
   into 4 equal pieces

¾ lb (375 g) Concord or Red Flame
   grapes, halved and seeded,
   if necessary

1 shallot, minced

1 tablespoon chopped fresh mint

splash of balsamic vinegar

New England has long been proud of its stock of farm-raised game birds, and bobwhite quail is often considered the finest of all. Roasting these little birds on a bed of local Concord grapes provides a perfect foil for their delicate meat. Serve with rice and a few watercress sprigs or sautéed greens.

1. Preheat the oven to 400°F (200°C).

2. Rinse the quail inside and out and pat dry with paper towels. Rub the birds with 1 tablespoon of the olive oil and season inside and out with salt and pepper. Fold the wing tips under the back and simply truss each bird with an 8-inch (20-cm) length of kitchen string by first tying together the leg ends using the very middle of the length of string. Bring the 2 ends of string back along the sides of the bird, running them between the breast and legs, and then slip the strings under the folded wings and knot the ends on the backside of the bird. Cover the breast of each bird with a piece of pancetta or bacon.

3. Combine the grapes, shallot, mint, and the ½ teaspoon salt and ¼ teaspoon pepper in the bottom of a roasting pan. Toss to mix well and spread in the pan. Drizzle with the remaining 3 tablespoons olive oil. Arrange the quail on top of the grapes.

4. Roast the quail until the juices run clear when a thigh joint is pricked with a fork, about 25 minutes. Remove from the oven and let the quail rest for about 5 minutes.

5. Remove the strings from the quail and pour any juices accumulated in the cavities onto the grapes. Add the balsamic vinegar. Place 2 quail per person on each individual plate and surround with the roasted grapes. Serve immediately.

SERVES 4

NUTRITIONAL ANALYSIS PER SERVING
Calories 820 (Kilojoules 3,444); Protein 61 g; Carbohydrates 15 g; Total Fat 57 g; Saturated Fat 15 g; Cholesterol 238 mg; Sodium 530 mg; Dietary Fiber 2 g

Stove-Top Clambake

1 lb (500 g) small red potatoes, unpeeled, halved or quartered

2 lb (1 kg) hard-shell clams such as littleneck or Maine mahogany, well scrubbed

2 qt (2 l) rockweed (seaweed), rinsed (optional)

4 live lobsters, 1–1¼ lb (500–625 g) each

4 ears of corn, husks and silk removed

1 cup (8 oz/250 g) butter, melted and kept warm

Here's an adaptation of the traditional outdoor clambake that brings the sweet scent of steamed clams and lobster into your kitchen. Ask your fishmonger for a bit of rockweed, the brownish green tangle of seaweed used to pack lobsters, and add it to your pot. It will add a nice "kiss" of saltwater.

1. In a saucepan, combine the potatoes with salted water to cover. Bring to a boil over high heat, then reduce the heat to medium. Simmer for 5 minutes. Drain and set aside.

2. Lay a double layer of cheesecloth (muslin) about 15 inches (38 cm) square on a work surface. Discard any clams that are gaping and do not close when tapped. Arrange half of the clams on the cloth and fold to make a flat, somewhat loose bundle. Tie the ends with kitchen string. Repeat with the remaining clams, and then make a third bundle with the potatoes.

3. Outfit a large lobster kettle or preserving kettle with a steamer rack that stands several inches above the bottom of the kettle. Pour in water to a depth of 1–2 inches (2.5–5 cm). Cover and bring to a boil over high heat, then turn off the heat. If using the rockweed, arrange a thin layer on the steamer rack. Set the lobsters on top, arrange the bundles of potatoes and clams on the lobsters, and then cover with another layer of rockweed. Cover, bring to a rapid boil, and cook everything for 16–18 minutes. After 8 minutes, lift the lid and set the ears of corn on top. Check for doneness by using tongs to see if the clams have opened. The lobsters should be bright red, and the steam should carry the sweet smell of cooked lobster.

4. Using the tongs, remove everything from the kettle, discard the rockweed, and pile the food onto a large platter. Snip open the bundles and discard any clams that failed to open. Divide the butter among warmed individual ramekins. Serve immediately, along with tools for cracking the lobster shells and plenty of napkins.

SERVES 4

NUTRITIONAL ANALYSIS PER SERVING
Calories 757 (Kilojoules 3,179); Protein 35 g; Carbohydrates 50 g; Total Fat 49 g; Saturated Fat 29 g; Cholesterol 217 mg; Sodium 945 mg; Dietary Fiber 6 g

In the late nineteenth century, well-to-do urbanites discovered the appeal of vacationing on the North Atlantic coast. The craggy beaches, the bracing sea-salt spray, and the abundance of fresh seafood offered relief from the bustle of city life—not unlike today. To satisfy their guests' appetites for an authentic taste of New England, restaurateurs and hoteliers staged clambakes and shore dinners, thus creating two seaside traditions that endure today.

The clambake, the more rustic of the pair, is an adaptation of the Native American tradition of cooking in a stone-lined pit. Once the shoreside pit is heated with hot coals, copious amounts of clams, corn, potatoes, and rockweed (a common seaweed with little bubbles of air that release steam when heated) go into it. Personal and regional variations abound, and clambakes may also include lobster, mussels, chicken, sausage, boiling onions, and even sweet potatoes. The pit is covered with canvas tarps and left to steam until everything is cooked through and saturated with a salty aroma.

A shore dinner, on the other hand, is a lavish sit-down affair served in a seaside restaurant or club dining

Clambakes

room. While menus vary according to the season and the locale, the best ones offer generous quantities of fresh seafood. These multicourse meals may include chowder, lobster stew, steamed clams, mussels, fried clams, fried scallops, baked cod, broiled sole, boiled lobster, potatoes, corn, rolls, plenty of sweet butter, salad, and fresh-baked pie.

Rubbed Steak with Asparagus

3 tablespoons sesame seeds, lightly toasted

3 tablespoons Asian sesame oil

2 tablespoons coriander seeds

2 teaspoons red pepper flakes

2 teaspoons brown sugar

1½ teaspoons coarse salt

3 tablespoons peeled and grated fresh ginger

2 cloves garlic, smashed and minced

1 tablespoon minced lemongrass

1 teaspoon soy sauce

4 rib-eye or strip steaks, each 8–10 oz (250–315 g) and 1 inch (2.5 cm) thick

1–1½ lb (500–750 g) asparagus, tough ends removed

1½ tablespoons olive oil or vegetable oil

New England hasn't been exempt from the wave of fusion cooking that has swept the country, and now many local dishes have an exotic accent. Prepare this recipe in late spring when the days are long and the asparagus is fat and tender.

1. Set aside 1 teaspoon each of the sesame seeds and sesame oil. In a mortar or spice grinder, grind together the remaining sesame seeds, the coriander seeds, red pepper flakes, brown sugar, and coarse salt. In a small bowl, mix the sesame seed mixture with the ginger, garlic, lemongrass, the remaining sesame oil, and ½ teaspoon of the soy sauce. Pat the steaks dry with paper towels and rub this mixture over the entire surface. Cover and refrigerate for at least 30 minutes or as long as 4 hours.

2. Prepare a medium-hot fire in a charcoal grill.

3. Brush the asparagus with a light coating of oil. Place the steaks on the grill rack and grill, turning once, for 5–8 minutes on each side for medium-rare or a minute or so longer for medium. Arrange the asparagus spears on the perimeter of the grill while the steaks cook and turn them often to brown them evenly. To check the steaks for doneness, make a small cut into the center of a steak with a paring knife. The steaks should be slightly less cooked than desired, as they will continue to cook a little more off the fire. When the steaks are done, transfer them to a platter and tent with aluminum foil.

4. Once the steaks are off the grill, shift the asparagus to the center of the grill rack where the fire is hottest and grill, turning as necessary, until tender and browned in spots, 4–5 minutes longer. Transfer the asparagus to a separate platter and season with the reserved 1 teaspoon each sesame seeds and sesame oil and the remaining ½ teaspoon soy sauce.

5. Uncover the steaks and serve with the asparagus immediately.

SERVES 4

NUTRITIONAL ANALYSIS PER SERVING
Calories 806 (Kilojoules 3,385); Protein 52 g; Carbohydrates 11 g; Total Fat 62 g; Saturated Fat 20 g; Cholesterol 157 mg; Sodium 765 mg; Dietary Fiber 3 g

Panfried Trout and Country Bacon

4 slices thick-cut bacon

4 whole trout, 8–10 oz (250–315 g)
  each, cleaned, or 4 trout fillets,
  6–8 oz (185–250 g) each

1 cup (8 fl oz/250 ml) milk

¾ cup (4 oz/125 g) yellow or white
  cornmeal

salt and freshly ground pepper
  to taste

¼ cup (2 fl oz/60 ml) peanut oil or
  vegetable oil

In addition to the bounty of fish and shellfish from the ocean, New England has its share of well-stocked trout streams and ponds. These trout make a fine supper, but they can also be a great way to wake up weekend guests. Serve with hash browns, sautéed apples, or johnnycakes (page 18) on the side.

1. Preheat the oven to 200°F (95°C).

2. In a large frying pan over medium heat, fry the bacon until crisp, about 8 minutes. Using tongs or a fork, transfer to paper towels to drain, then keep warm in the oven. Leave the drippings in the pan.

3. Rinse the fish under cold water and pat dry with paper towels. Put the milk and cornmeal in two separate shallow dishes. Season the cornmeal generously with salt and pepper. One at a time, dip the fish into the milk, and then roll them in the cornmeal to coat evenly.

4. Add the oil to the bacon drippings and place the frying pan over medium heat. When the fat is hot, lower the fish into the pan and fry them until their skin is crisp and golden, about 5 minutes for whole fish and 2 minutes for fillets. (If the pan isn't large enough to accommodate all the fish without their touching one another, cook in batches.) Using a spatula, gently turn the fish—be careful not to splatter yourself—and fry until opaque throughout, 3–5 minutes longer for whole fish and 1–2 minutes longer for fillets. Check for doneness by cutting into the thickest part of the fish to see if it is cooked through. (If cooking in batches, keep the first batch warm in the oven while you fry the rest.)

5. Transfer the fish to warmed individual plates and top each serving with a bacon slice. Serve at once.

SERVES 4

NUTRITIONAL ANALYSIS PER SERVING
Calories 718 (Kilojoules 3,016); Protein 48 g; Carbohydrates 23 g; Total Fat 47 g;
Saturated Fat 12 g; Cholesterol 145 mg; Sodium 379 mg; Dietary Fiber 1 g

Pot Roast with Hard Cider and Turnips

1 boneless beef chuck, top blade, or rump roast, 2½–3½ lb (1.25–1.75 kg), tied into a compact shape

1 teaspoon dried thyme

1 teaspoon freshly ground pepper

½ teaspoon coarse salt

½ teaspoon ground cinnamon

2 tablespoons vegetable oil or bacon drippings

1 large yellow onion, chopped into 1-inch (2.5-cm) pieces

2 carrots, peeled and chopped into 1-inch (2.5-cm) pieces

¾ cup (6 fl oz/180 ml) hard apple cider or dry apple wine

2 cloves garlic, chopped

1 bay leaf

¼ teaspoon allspice berries, lightly crushed

beef or chicken stock or water, if needed

1½ lb (750 g) small turnips, peeled and quartered

James Beard concluded that the Yankee pot roast was the creation of early French immigrants in Maine and New Hampshire.

1. Preheat the oven to 325°F (165°C).

2. Pat the surface of the roast dry with paper towels. In a small dish, stir together the thyme, pepper, coarse salt, and cinnamon. Rub the mixture over the meat. In a dutch oven or other ovenproof pot over high heat, warm the vegetable oil or bacon drippings until very hot. Add the roast and brown well on all sides, about 15 minutes. Transfer to a plate and set aside. Add the onion and carrots to the fat remaining in the pot and sauté, stirring, until beginning to brown, 3–4 minutes. Add the cider or wine, garlic, bay leaf, and allspice, and bring to a simmer. Using a wooden spoon, scrape the caramelized drippings from the pot bottom so they dissolve in the simmering liquid. Return the meat to the pot.

3. Cover the pot tightly, transfer to the oven, and roast the meat, turning it over every 30 minutes and adding some stock or water if the pot is dry, until it is tender enough to be easily pierced with a fork, 2–3 hours.

4. Meanwhile, bring a saucepan three-fourths full of salted water to a boil. Add the turnips and cook for 5 minutes. Drain and set aside.

5. When the meat is ready, transfer it to a serving platter. Snip the strings, and tent the meat with aluminum foil. Pour the pot liquid through a sieve into a vessel and skim the fat from the surface. Return the liquid to the pot and add the turnips. The liquid should almost cover the turnips; if not, add some stock or water. Bring to a simmer over medium-high heat and cook, shaking the pan once or twice to cook evenly, until tender, about 15 minutes. Adjust the seasonings.

6. Slice the meat and arrange it on a serving platter. Surround the meat with the turnips, and pour the pan juices over the meat and turnips.

SERVES 6

NUTRITIONAL ANALYSIS PER SERVING
Calories 622 (Kilojoules 2,612); Protein 42 g; Carbohydrates 13 g; Total Fat 44 g; Saturated Fat 16 g; Cholesterol 159 mg; Sodium 358 mg; Dietary Fiber 3 g

Despite their feisty independence and self-reliance, New Englanders love to join their neighbors and friends in church basements, Grange Halls, and meeting rooms for country suppers put on as fund-raisers for local congregations and other community groups. Menus vary from place to place, but whether it's baked ham or a fish fry, the accompaniments almost always include Parker House rolls, chopped salads, homemade pickles, and a lineup of pies and other homemade desserts. Drinks are rarely anything fancier than coffee, milk, or cider.

Yankees eat early, and most suppers begin around four o'clock. Some annual events have become so popular that several seatings are held to accommodate the hundreds of guests that are drawn by word of mouth and listings in local papers. Prices are always reasonable—between four and eight dollars for each adult—with reduced rates for children and seniors. Some groups even sell takeout plates for those folks who don't want to socialize even once a year.

No matter that the food is simple, the plates and utensils are typically plastic, and the tables and folded chairs are rented or borrowed, these

Church **Suppers**

suppers are the year's social and culinary highlight for many small towns. A sampling from around the region includes Chicken Pie Supper at the First Federated Church in Hudson, Massachusetts; Roast Beef Dinner at the Methodist Church in Bantam, Connecticut; and Yankee Pot Roast Dinner at the Grange Hall in Waterbury Center, Vermont.

Linguiça Sausage with Littleneck Clams

3 tablespoons olive oil

1 yellow onion, finely chopped

1 red or green bell pepper (capsicum), seeded and diced

¼ teaspoon coarse salt

pinch of red pepper flakes (optional)

2 or 3 cloves garlic, minced

1 teaspoon sweet paprika

1 lb (500 g) linguiça or other smoked pork sausage such as kielbasa, sliced ¼ inch (6 mm) thick

½ cup (4 fl oz/125 ml) dry white wine

1 can (28 oz/875 g) plum (Roma) tomatoes, drained and chopped

24 littleneck clams, about 2 lb (1 kg) total weight, well scrubbed

2 tablespoons chopped fresh flat-leaf (Italian) parsley

The industrious port city of New Bedford, Massachusetts, has been home to many Portuguese immigrants since the early nineteenth century, a fact reflected in the prevalence of gutsy recipes like this one. Serve the clams and sausage with crusty bread or over rice.

1. In a wide saucepan or large, deep frying pan over medium-low heat, warm the olive oil. Add the onion, bell pepper, coarse salt, and the red pepper flakes, if using, and cook, stirring often, until soft, about 15 minutes. Add the garlic and paprika and cook, stirring, for 1 minute longer. Stir in the sausage and cook, stirring occasionally, until heated through, 2–3 minutes.

2. Raise the heat to high and add the wine and tomatoes. Bring to a simmer and cook for 5 minutes to blend the flavors. Discard any clams that are gaping and do not close when tapped. Add the clams, cover, and cook until the clams open, which will take 6–10 minutes. The clams may not all open at the same time. As they do open, scoop them out with a slotted spoon and set them aside in a large bowl. After 10 minutes, pull out any clams that failed to open and discard.

3. Return the cooked clams, still in their shells, to the pan. Spoon into warmed pasta bowls and sprinkle with the chopped parsley. Serve immediately with forks and spoons.

SERVES 4

NUTRITIONAL ANALYSIS PER SERVING
Calories 552 (Kilojoules 2,318); Protein 22 g; Carbohydrates 18 g; Total Fat 42 g; Saturated Fat 13 g; Cholesterol 88 mg; Sodium 1,659 mg; Dietary Fiber 3 g

Turkey Croquettes

1 small yellow onion, chopped

1 celery stalk with leaves, chopped

3 tablespoons unsalted butter

1 cup (5 oz/155 g) all-purpose (plain) flour

1 cup (8 fl oz/250 ml) milk or chicken stock

2 cups (12 oz/375 g) chopped, skinless cooked turkey

1 teaspoon fresh lemon juice

½ teaspoon salt

¼ teaspoon sweet paprika

2 eggs, lightly beaten with a few drops of water

1 cup (4 oz/125 g) fine dried bread crumbs

vegetable oil for deep-frying

These croquettes are so delectable that I don't wait for Thanksgiving leftovers. Instead, I poach some fresh turkey (or chicken) whenever I crave them. Serve with cranberry sauce, if you like.

1. In a food processor, combine the onion and celery and pulse to chop finely. In a saucepan over medium-low heat, melt the butter. Add the chopped vegetables and cook, stirring often, until starting to soften, about 5 minutes. Stir in 3 tablespoons of the flour and cook, stirring, for 1 minute. Whisk in the milk or stock and simmer, stirring often, until the sauce is quite thick and smooth, 6–8 minutes. Remove from the heat.

2. Put the turkey into the food processor and pulse to chop finely. Add the turkey to the sauce and add the lemon juice, salt, and paprika. Pour the turkey mixture into a shallow baking dish, press a piece of plastic wrap directly onto the surface, and refrigerate until firm, 2–3 hours.

3. Preheat the oven to 200°F (95°C). Put the eggs and bread crumbs into 2 separate shallow bowls. Put the remaining flour on a work surface. Using a ¼-cup (2–fl oz/60-ml) measure, scoop up some of the turkey mixture and drop it onto the flour. Dip your fingers in the flour and shape the mixture into a patty, a rectangle, or even a small pyramid (the classic shape). Dip the croquette first into the egg and then roll in the bread crumbs to coat evenly. Place on a sheet of waxed paper. Repeat until all the turkey mixture is used up. You should have 8 croquettes.

4. Pour oil to a depth of about 2 inches (5 cm) into a heavy saucepan and heat to 375°F (190°C) on a deep-frying thermometer. Lower 4 croquettes into the oil and fry, turning as necessary, until browned on all sides, about 3 minutes total. Using a slotted spoon, transfer to paper towels to drain, then place in the oven while you fry the remaining croquettes.

5. Arrange the croquettes on a platter and serve piping hot.

MAKES 8 CROQUETTES; SERVES 4

NUTRITIONAL ANALYSIS PER SERVING
Calories 686 (Kilojoules 2,881); Protein 46 g; Carbohydrates 54 g; Total Fat 31 g; Saturated Fat 11 g; Cholesterol 225 mg; Sodium 691 mg; Dietary Fiber 3 g

Venison Stew with Beer and Onions

1–2 tablespoons unsalted butter, or as needed

2 slices thick-cut bacon, cut into ½-inch (12-mm) pieces

2 lb (1 kg) boneless venison stew meat, cut into 1½-inch (4-cm) cubes *(see note)*

salt and freshly ground pepper to taste

3 large yellow onions, thickly sliced

3 tablespoons all-purpose (plain) flour

2 tablespoons tomato paste

1 bottle (12 fl oz/375 ml) dark beer, preferably porter or stout

1 cup (8 fl oz/250 ml) beef, veal, or chicken stock

4 cloves garlic, chopped

1 strip orange zest, 3 inches (7.5 cm) long and ½ inch (12 mm) wide

1 bay leaf

2 fresh sage sprigs

1 tablespoon white wine vinegar

I like to imagine a triumphant hunter concocting this deeply flavored stew from what is on hand at deer camp: venison, beer, and onions. If venison is unavailable, use beef chuck, rump, or bottom round. Serve with buttered egg noodles or crusty bread. The stew is even better reheated the next day.

1. Preheat the oven to 325°F (165°C).

2. In a dutch oven or other heavy ovenproof pot with a tight-fitting lid, melt 1 tablespoon of the butter over medium heat. Add the bacon and cook until crisp, about 5 minutes. Using a slotted spoon, transfer the bacon to a plate and set aside.

3. Pat the venison dry with paper towels and season with salt and pepper. Working in batches, add the venison to the drippings remaining in the pot over medium-high heat. Brown quickly, turning to color on all sides. Do not crowd the pot or the meat will steam rather than brown. Using the slotted spoon, transfer the venison to the plate holding the bacon. If the pot seems dry, add another tablespoon of butter. When it melts, add the onions and sauté, stirring, until fragrant and just softened, 6–8 minutes. Season with salt and pepper. Stir in the flour and tomato paste and add the beer and stock. Bring to a simmer and deglaze the pan, scraping up any browned bits from the pot bottom. Add the garlic, orange zest, bay leaf, and sage sprigs and return the venison and bacon to the pot. Cover the pot and transfer to the oven. Cook gently until the meat is very tender, 1½–2 hours.

4. Remove the pot from the oven, uncover, and skim off any fat from the surface. Discard the orange zest, bay leaf, and sage sprigs. Add the vinegar, then taste and adjust the seasonings.

5. Ladle the stew into soup plates to serve.

SERVES 6

NUTRITIONAL ANALYSIS PER SERVING
Calories 356 (Kilojoules 1,495); Protein 38 g; Carbohydrates 17 g; Total Fat 14 g; Saturated Fat 6 g; Cholesterol 145 mg; Sodium 351 mg; Dietary Fiber 2 g

I n 1941, Aristene Pixley wrote *The Green Mountain Cookbook,* in which she extolled the merits of salt pork and milk gravy in typically restrained Yankee fashion: "Sliced thin, fried till crisp, and served with baked potatoes and 'milk gravy' made in the pan in which the pork was fried, it is not a dish to be disdained." Although the days of every homestead's having its own barrel of brine-cured pork are long past, contemporary New Englanders continue to share Pixley's sentiment.

At the outset, the pairing of salt pork and milk gravy was a dish born of economy. When the larder was nearly empty and all that remained were a few chunks of cured fatback, known as salt pork, a thrifty cook could turn these slightly briny, mostly fatty pieces of meat into a hearty meal by frying them up and serving them with a thick, creamy gravy made from the savory drippings, a handful of white flour, and a few cups of milk.

While few New Englanders live on such meager rations today, this simple country supper remains a favorite in homes and family-style restaurants across the northern reaches of Vermont, New Hampshire,

Salt Pork and **Milk Gravy**

and Maine. The Wayside Restaurant, a popular spot that has been serving home-style food on the road between Barre and Montpelier, Vermont, since 1918, is just one example of this tradition. Every week it still draws large crowds for its Thursday night special of fried salt pork slathered with thick, almost sweet milk gravy and served with potatoes and biscuits.

Holiday Oyster Stew

6 tablespoons (3 oz/90 g) unsalted
  butter

1 shallot, grated

2 pt (1 l) freshly shucked oysters
  with their liquid

2 cups (16 fl oz/500 ml) heavy
  (double) cream

1 cup (8 fl oz/250 ml) milk

few drops of Tabasco or other
  hot-pepper sauce

salt to taste

2 tablespoons finely chopped fresh
  chervil or chives (optional)

If you're up to the task of shucking the oysters yourself, figure four to five dozen medium-sized oysters for this recipe. I especially like the briny flavor of Atlantic oysters such as Wellfleets or Belons, which are harvested in the cold coastal waters of Maine.

1. Preheat the oven to 200°F (95°C). Place individual soup bowls on a baking sheet. Using about 1 tablespoon of the butter, place a sliver of butter in each bowl and slip the baking sheet into the oven.

2. Select a wide saucepan or deep sauté pan that will accommodate the oysters snugly in a single layer. Add the remaining 5 tablespoons (2½ oz/75 g) butter to the pan and place it over medium heat. When the butter melts, stir in the shallot and cook for a minute or two without browning. Add the oysters and their liquid, and heat until the liquid just starts to simmer and the edges of the oysters begin to curl, 2–5 minutes. Using a slotted spoon, transfer the oysters to a shallow bowl and set aside.

3. Raise the heat to high and cook the liquid until it is reduced by about half, 5–7 minutes. Add the cream and milk and bring to just below a boil. Taste and season discreetly with the Tabasco and salt. (The stew may be plenty salty from the oysters.) Reduce the heat to medium-low and return the oysters to the pan to heat through. Do not allow the stew to boil or stay too long on the heat, or the oysters will toughen.

4. Ladle into the warmed bowls and garnish each serving with a bit of chervil or chives, if desired. Serve piping hot.

SERVES 6–8

NUTRITIONAL ANALYSIS PER SERVING
Calories 443 (Kilojoules 1,861); Protein 13 g; Carbohydrates 9 g; Total Fat 40 g;
Saturated Fat 23 g; Cholesterol 204 mg; Sodium 207 mg; Dietary Fiber 0 g

Marjoram-and-Sage-Studded Pork Roast

1 tablespoon chopped fresh sage

1 tablespoon chopped fresh marjoram
   or oregano

1 clove garlic, minced

½ teaspoon dry mustard

½ teaspoon coarse salt

½ teaspoon freshly ground black
   pepper

⅛ teaspoon cayenne pepper

⅛ teaspoon ground nutmeg

1 bone-in pork loin roast, 3–4 lb
   (1.5–2 kg), backbone cracked

2 teaspoons olive oil

about 2 cups (16 fl oz/500 ml) dry
   white wine, chicken stock, or water

2 tablespoons unsalted butter
   (optional)

Gone are the days when every New England homestead raised a few fat pigs to provide meat for the family, but pork remains popular across the region. Ask your butcher to crack the backbone to make carving easy.

1. In a small bowl, stir together the sage, the marjoram or oregano, garlic, mustard, coarse salt, black pepper, cayenne, and nutmeg. With the tip of a sharp paring knife, make 15–20 small slits all over the pork roast. Stuff small pinches of some of the herb mixture into the slits. Rub the roast with the olive oil and spread the remaining herb mixture over the surface of the meat. Cover with plastic wrap and refrigerate for 2–6 hours.

2. Preheat the oven to 450°F (230°C).

3. Set the roast, bone side down, in a roasting pan. Roast for 10 minutes, then reduce the oven temperature to 275°F (135°C) and pour 1 cup (8 fl oz/250 ml) of the wine, stock, or water over the roast. Continue to roast, checking from time to time and adding more liquid if the pan is completely dry, until an instant-read thermometer inserted into the thickest part away from the bone registers 155°F (68°C), about 2 hours. Transfer to a carving board, tent with aluminum foil, and let rest for 10–15 minutes.

4. If you would like to make a simple pan sauce, skim off any fat from the pan juices in the roasting pan and set it on the stove top over medium-high heat. If there is less than ½ cup (4 fl oz/125 ml) pan drippings remaining, add ½ cup (4 fl oz/125 ml) of the wine, stock, or water. Bring to a boil and deglaze the pan, stirring to scrape up any browned bits stuck to the pan bottom. Whisk in the butter, if using. Season to taste with salt and pepper. Pour into a warmed bowl or gravy boat.

5. Carve the roast into ¼–½-inch (6–12-mm) slices and arrange on a warmed platter. Pass the pan sauce at the table.

SERVES 6

NUTRITIONAL ANALYSIS PER SERVING
Calories 426 (Kilojoules 1,789); Protein 43 g; Carbohydrates 1 g; Total Fat 25 g;
Saturated Fat 9 g; Cholesterol 130 mg; Sodium 210 mg; Dietary Fiber 0 g

Corn .30 ear $3.50 dozen
Native Tomatoes $2.00 lb
Beans $1.00 lb
Cabbage green 5/1.00
Potatoes .75 g/LB
Red cabbage 30¢/LB
Squash .30 lb 5 LBs/1.00
Peppers .75 lb
Broccoli 1.00 lb
Onions 40/LB 3 3@$1.00
Cucumbers 5/1.00
Lettuce .75 each 3/$2.00
Cutflower Bouquets $2.00 ea

3 Vegetables, Grains & Beans

As much as the landscape changes with the seasons in New England, so do the vegetables and side dishes on the table at dinnertime. In the spring, few cooks can resist the fresh taste of asparagus, fiddleheads, and peas. By summer, we clamor for the fleeting taste of ripe tomatoes, corn, greens, and fresh herbs. Then as fall encroaches, we happily fortify ourselves with hearty winter squashes and long-keeping root vegetables. And finally, in the depths of winter, we are thankful for the dried beans and grains that comfort us against the cold.

Roasted Beets with Herbs and Vinegar

1½ lb (750 g) uniform-sized beets
  (2 lb/1 kg with greens attached)

1½ teaspoons olive oil

½ cup (2 oz/60 g) walnut pieces
  (optional)

1½ tablespoons unsalted butter or
  extra-virgin olive oil

2 tablespoons chopped fresh chervil,
  chives, parsley, or tarragon

1 tablespoon sherry vinegar or
  balsamic vinegar, or to taste

salt and freshly ground pepper
  to taste

This dish was inspired by my father, who, despite allegiance to his alma mater, can't stand the sticky-sweet dressing on traditional Harvard beets. The rich crimson of these popular root vegetables is speckled with green herbs, making an appealing side dish for red meat or poultry.

1. Preheat the oven to 400°F (200°C).

2. If the greens are still attached to the beets, cut them off and reserve for another use. Leave the root and ½ inch (12 mm) of the stem intact on each beet and scrub the beets well. Dry with paper towels, then rub with the olive oil. Wrap the beets together in a large piece of heavy-duty aluminum foil, sealing the foil closed to make a tight packet so no juices leak out during roasting. Put the packet on a baking sheet.

3. Roast the beets until tender, 45–90 minutes. The timing will depend on the size of the beets. To test for doneness, poke a small knife through the foil into a beet. It should pierce into the vegetable easily.

4. Meanwhile, if using the walnuts, spread them in a pie pan and place in the oven with the beets. Toast the nuts, watching carefully so they do not burn, until they take on color and are fragrant, 8–10 minutes. Remove from the oven and set aside to cool.

5. When the beets are ready, remove them from the oven, discard the foil, and let the beets cool until they can be handled, 8–10 minutes. Using a paring knife, trim off the stems and slip off the skins. Cut the beets into wedges or thick slices and put them in a bowl.

6. Add the butter or extra-virgin olive oil, herb, and the walnuts, if using, to the beets and toss well. Season with the vinegar, salt, and pepper and toss again. Transfer to a serving bowl and serve the beets warm.

SERVES 4

NUTRITIONAL ANALYSIS PER SERVING
Calories 106 (Kilojoules 445); Protein 2 g; Carbohydrates 12 g; Total Fat 6 g;
Saturated Fat 3 g; Cholesterol 12 mg; Sodium 87 mg; Dietary Fiber 1 g

Fresh Stirred Corn with Chives

8 ears of corn, husks and silk removed

¼ teaspoon coarse salt, plus salt
   to taste

2 tablespoons chopped fresh chives

freshly ground pepper to taste

1 tablespoon unsalted butter (optional)

Baked corn pudding enriched with cream and eggs is a popular New England holiday indulgence. In the summer, however, when sweet corn is at its peak, there's nothing better than this simple preparation—a recipe told to me across the counter at my local farm stand. It goes with everything from grilled hamburgers to roast lamb.

1. With the tip of a sharp knife, score the kernels of an ear of corn by drawing the tip of the knife down the center of each row. Then stand the ear upright on a plate or in a shallow bowl and scrape a spoon down each row, applying enough pressure to remove all of the pulp and juices, leaving behind the kernel skins. Repeat with the remaining ears. You should have about 3 cups (18 oz/560 g) of very milky corn.

2. Put the corn in a saucepan, preferably nonstick, and place over medium heat. Add the ¼ teaspoon salt and bring to a simmer. Cook, stirring often with a wooden spoon, until about one-third of the liquid has evaporated and the corn is the consistency of thick porridge, 8–10 minutes. The corn will bubble and sputter, but it should not boil vigorously. If you are not using a nonstick pan, a brown crust will form on the bottom and sides of the pan. Do not try to scrape this off to mix it with the corn. Instead, simply stir the corn without breaking up the crust. This crust will protect the corn from burning while infusing it with a toasty flavor.

3. Stir in the chives, pepper, and the butter, if using. Taste and adjust the seasonings.

4. Spoon into a warmed bowl and serve immediately.

SERVES 4

NUTRITIONAL ANALYSIS PER SERVING
Calories 248 (Kilojoules 1,042); Protein 9 g; Carbohydrates 55 g; Total Fat 3 g; Saturated Fat 1 g; Cholesterol 0 mg; Sodium 134 mg; Dietary Fiber 9 g

Baked Beans with Molasses

2 rounded cups (1 lb/500 g) navy beans or other dried white beans

½ cup (5½ oz/170 g) molasses

¼ cup (3 oz/90 g) maple syrup or (2 oz/60 g) firmly packed brown sugar

2 tablespoons dark rum (optional)

2 teaspoons dry mustard

1½ teaspoons coarse salt

1 teaspoon freshly ground pepper

3 cups (24 fl oz/750 ml) water

6 oz (185 g) lean salt pork

1 bay leaf

1 yellow onion

2 or 3 whole cloves

Boston earned its sobriquet Beantown because of the Puritans, who made a pot of beans every Saturday to last through Sunday, their day of rest. Serve these robust beans with brown bread and coleslaw for supper or as a welcome side dish at any barbecue.

1. Pick over the beans and discard any stones or misshapen beans. Rinse the beans, place in a large bowl, and add water to cover by 3 inches (7.5 cm). Let soak for at least 8 hours or as long as overnight. Drain well.

2. Preheat the oven to 275°F (135°C).

3. In a saucepan, stir together the molasses, maple syrup or brown sugar, rum (if using), mustard, coarse salt, pepper, and water. Place over medium heat and bring to a simmer, stirring to combine the ingredients. Immediately remove from the heat and set aside.

4. Trim off the rind from the salt pork, keeping it in one piece, and cut the pork into ½-inch (12-mm) cubes. Put the rind in the bottom of a 2½–3-qt (2.5–3-l) dutch oven or earthenware bean pot. Attach the bay leaf to the whole onion, using the cloves as tacks. Add it to the pot. Then add the beans and the salt pork. Pour the molasses mixture evenly over the top. The beans should be completely immersed in the liquid; if not, add enough water to cover. Place the lid on the pot, securing a tight fit.

5. Bake for 5 hours, checking every hour to see that the top is still moist. If it is not, add a little more water. After 5 hours, increase the oven temperature to 300°F (150°C), remove the lid, and lift out and discard the onion. Continue to bake, uncovered, stirring gently every 15 minutes or so, until the beans are very tender, about 1 hour longer.

6. Discard the pork rind and serve the beans hot directly from the pot. Leftovers can be refrigerated for up to a week and reheated to serve.

SERVES 6 AS A MAIN COURSE, OR 10–12 AS A SIDE DISH

NUTRITIONAL ANALYSIS PER SERVING
Calories 552 (Kilojoules 2,318); Protein 19 g; Carbohydrates 76 g; Total Fat 20 g; Saturated Fat 7 g; Cholesterol 20 mg; Sodium 727 mg; Dietary Fiber 8 g

From the communal iron pot of boiled smoked meats, salted fish, and hardtack biscuits that nourished the earliest settlers during their arduous transatlantic crossing to today's weeknight macaroni-and-cheese casserole, Yankee cooking has a rich heritage of one-pot meals. In contrast to the Southern tradition of abundant side dishes, the archetypal New England meal is a comforting stew, chowder, braise, pot roast, or casserole. Born of thrift and Puritan ethics, these simple, hearty dishes require no fussing and are provincially referred to as "made" dishes. They economize on both fuel and effort, as they can be left to simmer slowly on the back of a stove (originally the woodstove, now quite often a low oven) for hours, leaving the cook free to complete other chores. This is also an ideal way to coax tough cuts of meat, poultry, and even seafood such as chowder clams to tenderness.

Possibly the most renowned, and enduring, one-pot meal of all time is Boston baked beans. Simply made with navy beans, salt pork, molasses or maple syrup, and onions, baked beans are typically cooked in a bean pot, a stoneware vessel with a small

One-Pot Meals

top and bulging sides designed to minimize evaporation and retain heat long after the beans are cooked.

Another favorite category of "made" dishes is savory meat pies, including shepherd's pie, turkey pot pie, Hartley's pork pie from Fall River, Massachusetts, and French-Canadian tourtière (pastry-wrapped pork pâté).

Baked Macaroni and Sharp Cheddar

1 lb (500 g) dried ziti, shells, or
   elbow macaroni

6 tablespoons (3 oz/90 g) unsalted
   butter

1 small yellow onion, finely chopped

¼ cup (1½ oz/45 g) all-purpose
   (plain) flour

3 cups (24 fl oz/750 ml) milk

1 bay leaf

1 fresh thyme sprig

2 cups shredded sharp cheddar cheese

¾ teaspoon salt

¼ teaspoon freshly ground pepper

¼ teaspoon dry mustard

½ cup (1 oz/30 g) fresh bread crumbs

Once referred to as macaroni pudding in parts of Connecticut, this timeless dish shows up at nearly every church supper and potluck, as well as on home supper tables. Add some diced ham, sautéed mushrooms, caramelized onions, or a different cheese to dress it up.

1. Preheat the oven to 375°F (190°C). Butter a 3-qt (3-l) baking dish.

2. Bring a large pot three-fourths full of salted water to a boil. Add the pasta, stir well, and boil until almost tender. The timing will depend upon the type of pasta. Remember, it will cook in the oven, so do not overcook it now. Drain, rinse briefly under cold water, and place in a large bowl.

3. Meanwhile, melt 4 tablespoons (2 oz/60 g) of the butter in a saucepan over low heat. Add the onion and cook gently, stirring often, until softened, about 5 minutes. Stir in the flour and cook, stirring, for 1 minute to make a blond paste. Whisking continuously, add the milk a little at a time, being careful not to let any lumps form. Add the bay leaf and thyme sprig and bring to a simmer. Continue simmering, whisking occasionally, until the sauce is quite smooth and thick, about 15 minutes.

4. Remove the bay leaf and thyme sprig from the sauce and discard. Stir in the cheese until it melts, but do not allow the sauce to come to a boil. Stir in the salt, pepper, and mustard.

5. Pour the sauce over the pasta and toss well. Transfer to the prepared baking dish. In a small saucepan over low heat, melt the remaining 2 tablespoons butter. Remove from the heat, add the bread crumbs, and mix well. Sprinkle the buttered crumbs evenly over the pasta.

6. Bake the macaroni until it is bubbly and nicely browned on top, 35–45 minutes. Remove from the oven and let stand for 5 minutes. Serve with a large serving spoon.

SERVES 8 AS A SIDE DISH, OR 4–6 AS A MAIN COURSE

NUTRITIONAL ANALYSIS PER SERVING
Calories 496 (Kilojoules 2,083); Protein 18 g; Carbohydrates 54 g; Total Fat 23 g;
Saturated Fat 14 g; Cholesterol 67 mg; Sodium 661 mg; Dietary Fiber 2 g

Dandelion Greens with Garlic and White Wine

3 tablespoons olive oil or bacon
    drippings

3 cloves garlic, thinly sliced

¼ teaspoon red pepper flakes

1 large bunch dandelion greens,
    about 1 lb (500 g), tough stems
    removed and leaves cut into 2-inch
    (5-cm) lengths

salt and freshly ground black pepper
    to taste

1 cup (8 fl oz/250 ml) chicken stock

½ cup (4 fl oz/125 ml) dry white wine

1 tablespoon balsamic vinegar

At the first hint of spring, locals greedily forage for young, tender dandelion shoots. Later in the season, the yellow flower buds are collected for dandelion tempura. Fortunately, many markets sell cultivated dandelions, which make a fine substitute for their wild kin, as do kale and collards.

1. In a large frying pan over medium heat, warm together the olive oil or bacon drippings, garlic, and red pepper flakes until fragrant and the garlic starts to soften, 2–3 minutes. Add the dandelion greens and season with salt and black pepper. Raise the heat to high and toss the leaves with tongs to coat them with the oil.

2. Add the stock and wine, cover, and reduce the heat to medium-low. Simmer until the leaves are very tender and their flavor has mellowed, 30–40 minutes. Uncover, raise the heat to high, and boil for a few minutes to evaporate most of the remaining liquid. Add the balsamic vinegar and cook for 1 minute longer.

3. Transfer the dandelion greens to a warmed serving dish and serve immediately.

SERVES 4

NUTRITIONAL ANALYSIS PER SERVING
Calories 148 (Kilojoules 622); Protein 3 g; Carbohydrates 11 g; Total Fat 11 g;
Saturated Fat 1 g; Cholesterol 0 mg; Sodium 330 mg; Dietary Fiber 4 g

Pan-Glazed Parsnips with Sherry

1 lb (500 g) parsnips, peeled

½ cup (4 fl oz/125 ml) chicken stock
  or water

2 tablespoons unsalted butter

2 tablespoons dry sherry or Madeira

2 teaspoons peeled and minced fresh
  ginger

1 teaspoon chopped fresh thyme,
  or ¼ teaspoon dried

salt to taste

few drops of fresh lemon juice

freshly ground pepper to taste

The town of Westfield, Massachusetts, is the self-appointed Parsnip Capital of the World, and in fact these sweet and flavorful root vegetables are favored throughout the region. Real connoisseurs prefer spring-dug parsnips, which grow sweeter after a winter in the frozen ground.

1. Cut the parsnips in half lengthwise, then cut the halves in half again if they are very thick. Cut the pieces in half crosswise so you have finger-length sticks that are more or less the same thickness. If the cores are distinctly darker and denser than the rest of the root, remove them with a paring knife. These tough cores result from long storage and will remain fibrous even after cooking. Freshly dug parsnips will have tender cores that do not need to be removed.

2. Lay the parsnips in a frying pan large enough to accommodate them in a single layer. Add the stock or water, butter, sherry or Madeira, ginger, and thyme. Season with salt. Partially cover the pan and place over medium heat. Bring to a simmer and cook until the parsnips are tender enough to easily pierce with the tip of a knife, 7–9 minutes.

3. Uncover the pan, raise the heat to high, and continue to cook, uncovered, until the juices are reduced to a glaze, 4–6 minutes. Season with the lemon juice and a few grinds of pepper. Taste and adjust the seasonings.

4. Transfer the parsnips to a warmed serving dish and serve immediately.

SERVES 3 OR 4

NUTRITIONAL ANALYSIS PER SERVING
Calories 189 (Kilojoules 794); Protein 2 g; Carbohydrates 24 g; Total Fat 8 g;
Saturated Fat 5 g; Cholesterol 21 mg; Sodium 182 mg; Dietary Fiber 6 g

Scalloped Potatoes and Leeks

2 lb (1 kg) Yukon gold or other all-purpose potatoes, peeled and sliced ⅛ inch (3 mm) thick

1 small leek, including tender green part, finely chopped

1 teaspoon chopped fresh thyme, or ¼ teaspoon dried

salt and freshly ground pepper to taste

1 tablespoon unsalted butter, cut into very small pieces

1 cup (8 fl oz/250 ml) half-and-half (half cream)

1 cup (8 fl oz/250 ml) chicken stock or milk

New Englanders scallop all manner of local ingredients by baking them slowly in cream or milk, but scalloped potatoes are arguably the most popular of the lot. Use an all-purpose variety, such as Yukon gold or the White Kennebecs and Katahdins from Maine.

1. Put a baking sheet on the lowest rack of the oven to catch any spills, and preheat the oven to 375°F (190°C). Butter a 2-qt (2-l) gratin dish or baking dish.

2. Layer half of the potatoes on the bottom of the prepared dish. Sprinkle with the chopped leek and thyme. Season liberally with salt and pepper and dot the top with half of the butter. Arrange the remaining potatoes in a layer on top. The dish should be no more than three-fourths full. Season the top with salt and pepper.

3. In a small saucepan over medium heat, combine the half-and-half and the stock or milk. Heat until small bubbles appear along the edges of the pan, then remove from the heat. Pour the mixture evenly over the potatoes. Dot the top with the remaining butter and cover tightly with aluminum foil.

4. Bake the potatoes for 40 minutes. Remove the foil and continue to bake until the top is golden and the potatoes are tender enough to be easily pierced with a knife, 35–40 minutes longer. Remove from the oven and let stand for 10 minutes before serving. Scoop out the potatoes with a large spoon or spatula to serve.

SERVES 6

NUTRITIONAL ANALYSIS PER SERVING
Calories 178 (Kilojoules 748); Protein 4 g; Carbohydrates 24 g; Total Fat 8 g; Saturated Fat 5 g; Cholesterol 22 mg; Sodium 199 mg; Dietary Fiber 2 g

Fried Zucchini Blossoms

Ever since I tasted these fried blossoms in a restaurant in New Haven, Connecticut, I've grown zucchini primarily for the delicious flowers that emerge in early summer. The male blooms, the ones that grow on a stem and not on a zucchini, are best for frying because they have a firmer texture, but either can be used.

¾ cup (4 oz/125 g) all-purpose (plain) flour

½ teaspoon salt

¼ teaspoon freshly ground pepper

¼ teaspoon freshly grated nutmeg

1 cup (8 fl oz/250 ml) water

12 zucchini (courgette) or summer squash blossoms

vegetable oil for deep-frying

12 fresh sage leaves (optional)

1. In a bowl, whisk together the flour, salt, pepper, and nutmeg. Pour in the water and whisk briefly to form a thin batter. Do not overmix. Let the batter rest for 10–15 minutes.

2. If the blossoms appear dirty, rinse quickly and thoroughly pat dry with paper towels. Trim the stems, leaving ½ inch (12 mm) intact. Any very large blossoms should be cut in half lengthwise.

3. Preheat the oven to 200°F (95°C). Pour vegetable oil to a depth of 2–3 inches (5–7.5 cm) into a wide saucepan and heat to 370°F (188°C) on a deep-frying thermometer. When the oil is hot, dip the blossoms, one by one, into the batter and lower them into the oil. Work in batches, being careful not to crowd the pan; the blossoms should not touch while they are frying. Fry the blossoms, flipping once, until they are a pale ivory and crisp, 1–2 minutes total. Using tongs, transfer the blossoms to paper towels to drain. Keep warm in the oven while you fry the remaining blossoms.

4. If using the sage leaves, drop into the hot oil and fry briefly, 5–10 seconds. Scoop out with a slotted spoon and drain for a few moments on paper towels.

5. Arrange the blossoms on a warmed platter and scatter the sage leaves, if using, over the top. Serve immediately.

SERVES 4

NUTRITIONAL ANALYSIS PER SERVING
Calories 165 (Kilojoules 693); Protein 3 g; Carbohydrates 22 g; Total Fat 7 g;
Saturated Fat 1 g; Cholesterol 0 mg; Sodium 290 mg; Dietary Fiber 1 g

Pappardelle with Spring Vegetables

½ lb (250 g) fiddlehead ferns

1½ tablespoons unsalted butter
  or olive oil

6 oz (185 g) fresh morel or chanterelle
  mushrooms, brushed clean

salt and freshly ground pepper
  to taste

1 shallot, minced

1½ cups (12 fl oz/375 ml) chicken
  stock

½ lb (250 g) asparagus, tough ends
  removed and spears cut on the
  diagonal into 1½-inch (4-cm)
  lengths

½ cup (4 fl oz/125 ml) heavy (double)
  cream

few drops of fresh lemon juice

2 tablespoons chopped fresh chives,
  plus extra for garnish

¾ lb (375 g) fresh pappardelle or
  fettuccine

This is pasta primavera, New England style. If available, use fiddleheads, the tightly coiled fern shoots that pop up in the woods in the early spring. If you can't find them in your market, simply double the amount of asparagus.

1. Trim the tails (or stems) on the fiddleheads to about ½ inch (12 mm). Rinse the fiddleheads in a large basin or sink filled with water, sloshing them around to remove the bits of brown chaff that cling to the coils. Drain well.

2. Bring a large pot three-fourths full of water to a boil. Add the fiddleheads and blanch for 1–2 minutes. Drain and rinse under cold water to stop the cooking. Drain again.

3. Refill the pot three-fourths full of water and bring to a boil.

4. While the water is heating, in a large frying pan over medium heat, warm the butter or olive oil. Add the mushrooms and sauté, stirring often, until they soften but do not brown, about 5 minutes. Season with salt and pepper. Add the shallot and fiddleheads and cook for 1 minute longer. Add the stock and bring to a simmer. Stir in the asparagus and the cream and cook until the asparagus is tender, about 5 minutes. Add the lemon juice and the 2 tablespoons chives. Taste and adjust the seasonings.

5. Meanwhile, generously salt the boiling water and add the pasta. Stir well and cook until al dente, 2–3 minutes. Rinse a large bowl with hot water to heat it. Dry and set aside. Drain the pasta and transfer it to the warmed bowl. Pour the sauce onto the pasta and toss to coat.

6. Divide the pasta among warmed pasta bowls and garnish with chives. Serve immediately.

SERVES 4

NUTRITIONAL ANALYSIS PER SERVING
Calories 430 (Kilojoules 1,806); Protein 15 g; Carbohydrates 54 g; Total Fat 18 g;
Saturated Fat 10 g; Cholesterol 115 mg; Sodium 413 mg; Dietary Fiber 3 g

Smashed Winter Root Vegetables

1 large russet or Yukon gold potato, about 1 lb (500 g), peeled and cut into 1-inch (2.5-cm) chunks

2 lb (1 kg) root vegetables such as rutabaga, celeriac, parsnip, or carrot (a single vegetable or a mixture), peeled and cut into 1-inch (2.5-cm) chunks

1 teaspoon salt, plus salt to taste

3 tablespoons vegetable oil

3 shallots, about 3 oz (90 g) total weight, sliced into thin rounds

½ teaspoon sugar

¼ cup (2 oz/60 g) unsalted butter, cut into 4 equal pieces

pinch of freshly grated nutmeg

freshly ground pepper to taste

Because of the short growing season in the Northeast, many homes continue to rely on their root cellars to provide fresh vegetables throughout the winter. Whether made from a single type of vegetable or a combination of two or three, this side dish is a favorite accompaniment to roasts and stews.

1. In a saucepan, combine the potato and root vegetable(s), the 1 teaspoon salt, and water to cover. Place over high heat and bring to a boil. Immediately reduce the heat to medium and simmer rapidly, uncovered, until the vegetables are tender enough to mash on the side of the pot with a wooden spoon, 20–30 minutes.

2. Meanwhile, in a frying pan over high heat, warm the vegetable oil. Separate the shallot slices into rings and add to the oil. Fry, stirring often, until golden brown, 4–7 minutes. Add the sugar and a good pinch of salt, and cook for 1 minute longer. The shallots should be crisp and well colored. Using a slotted spoon, transfer the shallots to paper towels to drain, arranging them in a single layer.

3. When the vegetables are tender, drain them, reserving 1 cup (8 fl oz/ 250 ml) of the cooking liquid. Return the vegetables to the saucepan and, using a potato masher or large wooden spoon, mash them, adding the butter as you work. Add enough of the reserved cooking liquid to make a soft consistency. Season with the nutmeg, salt, and pepper.

4. Transfer the vegetables to a warmed serving dish and sprinkle with the crisp shallots. Serve immediately.

SERVES 6

NUTRITIONAL ANALYSIS PER SERVING
Calories 241 (Kilojoules 1,012); Protein 3 g; Carbohydrates 25 g; Total Fat 15 g; Saturated Fat 6 g; Cholesterol 21 mg; Sodium 324 mg; Dietary Fiber 4 g

Kedgeree

3 tablespoons unsalted butter or olive oil

1 yellow onion, finely chopped

2 teaspoons peeled and grated fresh ginger

2 cloves garlic, minced

2 teaspoons Madras curry powder

pinch of cayenne pepper

1½ cups (10½ oz/330 g) long-grain white rice, preferably basmati or jasmine

2½ cups (20 fl oz/625 ml) water

¾ teaspoon salt

2 large tomatoes, about 1 lb (500 g) total weight

½ lb (250 g) smoked trout fillets, skin removed and flaked into bite-sized pieces

3 tablespoons chopped fresh cilantro (fresh coriander) or green (spring) onion, including tender green tops

Kedgeree, a traditional breakfast dish of curried rice with smoked fish and cream, was brought to the colonies by British seafarers. This updated version uses tomatoes in place of the cream. It makes a marvelous brunch, light supper, or buffet dish.

1. In a heavy saucepan over medium-low heat, warm 2 tablespoons of the butter or olive oil. Add the onion and cook, stirring often, until softened, about 10 minutes. Add the ginger, garlic, curry, and cayenne, and cook, stirring, until the ginger and garlic are softened, about 3 minutes. Stir in the rice and cook, stirring, until the grains are well coated, about 2 minutes.

2. Pour in the water and add the salt. Raise the heat to high, and bring to a boil. Stir once, cover tightly, reduce the heat to low, and cook without stirring until the liquid is absorbed and the rice is tender, about 15 minutes. Remove from the heat and let the rice stand, covered, for 10 minutes.

3. Meanwhile, cut out the core of each tomato, then cut the tomato in half crosswise. Scoop out the seeds with your finger and chop the tomato into a rough dice. In a frying pan over medium heat, warm the remaining 1 tablespoon butter or olive oil. Add the flaked trout and cook, shaking the pan to cook evenly without breaking up the trout, until heated through, 2–3 minutes. Add the tomatoes and cook, stirring once or twice, just long enough to heat through but without letting the tomatoes turn mushy, 3–4 minutes.

4. Mound the rice onto a serving platter. Spoon the tomato-trout mixture on top and garnish with the cilantro or green onion. Serve hot, warm, or at room temperature.

SERVES 8-10 AS A SIDE DISH, OR 6 AS A MAIN COURSE

NUTRITIONAL ANALYSIS PER SERVING
Calories 210 (Kilojoules 882); Protein 10 g; Carbohydrates 30 g; Total Fat 7 g; Saturated Fat 3 g; Cholesterol 17 mg; Sodium 460 mg; Dietary Fiber 1 g

Fresh Peas with Prosciutto

Fresh garden peas simmered with salt pork and cream are a favorite summertime side dish for roast chicken or pork. This nondairy adaptation is much lighter but every bit as satisfying. If peas are out of season, use frozen petite peas and simply defrost them rather than boil them.

1. Fill a large pot three-fourths full of salted water and bring to a boil.

2. While the water is heating, in a large frying pan over low heat, warm the olive oil. Add the prosciutto and cook slowly, stirring often, until just heated through and slightly darker in color, 2–3 minutes. Be sure to keep the heat low and do not overcook the prosciutto, or it will toughen.

3. When the water is boiling, add the peas and boil for about 1 minute. The peas should be just barely tender. Drain immediately in a colander and dump the drained peas into the pan with the prosciutto. Raise the heat to medium and toss gently until the peas and prosciutto are well combined. Season with a few turns of the pepper mill, then taste to see if any salt is needed. The prosciutto may have contributed enough salt.

4. Transfer to a warmed serving dish and serve immediately.

SERVES 6

NUTRITIONAL ANALYSIS PER SERVING
Calories 109 (Kilojoules 458); Protein 7 g; Carbohydrates 10 g; Total Fat 5 g;
Saturated Fat 1 g; Cholesterol 8 mg; Sodium 307 mg; Dietary Fiber 3 g

1½ tablespoons extra-virgin olive oil

2 slices prosciutto, each about 1 oz (30 g) and ¹⁄₁₆ inch (2 mm) thick, cut into strips ⅛ inch (3 mm) wide

3 cups (15 oz/470 g) shelled English peas (about 3 lb/1.5 kg unshelled)

salt and freshly ground pepper to taste

Tomato and Summer Squash Gratin

1 lb (500 g) tomatoes, cut into slices
    ¼ inch (6 mm) thick

coarse salt to taste

3 tablespoons olive oil

2 cloves garlic, minced

1 zucchini (courgette), trimmed and
    cut into slices ¼ inch (6 mm) thick

1 yellow summer squash, trimmed
    and cut into slices ¼ inch (6 mm)
    thick

1 small yellow onion, very thinly
    sliced

freshly ground pepper to taste

1 teaspoon chopped fresh thyme

½ cup (2 oz/60 g) shredded sharp
    cheddar cheese

¼ cup (1 oz/30 g) grated Parmesan
    cheese

Gratins are favorite Yankee supper dishes all year round. Add a simple steak, pork chop, or chicken breast to this summertime version, and you've got a satisfying meal. Feel free to use other fresh herbs—basil, tarragon, marjoram, dill—in place of the thyme.

1. Sprinkle each tomato slice on both sides with coarse salt and arrange in a single layer in a colander or on a rack over a sink or bowl. Let drain for 35–45 minutes, then pat dry with paper towels.

2. Preheat the oven to 350°F (180°C). Brush the bottom and sides of a medium-sized oval gratin dish or a 7-by-11-inch (18-by-28-cm) baking dish with ½ tablespoon of the olive oil.

3. Scatter one-half of the garlic over the bottom of the prepared dish. Arrange a neat layer of the tomato, zucchini, yellow squash, and onion slices in the bottom of the dish, alternating the vegetables and overlapping the slices. Sprinkle the layer with coarse salt and pepper and with some of the garlic and thyme. (Be judicious with the salt as the tomatoes are already salted.) Make additional layers in the same manner until all the vegetables have been used and the dish is full. Sprinkle the surface with coarse salt, pepper, any remaining garlic and thyme, and then with the cheddar and Parmesan cheeses. Drizzle the remaining 2½ table-spoons olive oil evenly over the top.

4. Bake until nicely browned and most of the juices released by the vegetables have evaporated, 40–60 minutes. Remove from the oven and let stand for 5–10 minutes before serving.

SERVES 4

NUTRITIONAL ANALYSIS PER SERVING
Calories 230 (Kilojoules 966); Protein 9 g; Carbohydrates 12 g; Total Fat 17 g; Saturated Fat 6 g; Cholesterol 20 mg; Sodium 233 mg; Dietary Fiber 3 g

4 Desserts

The dessert repertoire of New England cooks is impressive and varied. From pies made with sweet summer fruits, to the raised fruit cakes once known as election cakes, to the comforting bread-and-butter puddings of wintertime, Yankees love their sweets—but never too sweet. Although these recipes are all grouped under the heading of desserts, such treats and confections show up just as often on the breakfast table or for an afternoon snack. In fact, the old-fashioned ice cream social is still very much alive and well in small-town life in the region.

Rhubarb-Strawberry-Ginger Pie

pie pastry (page 85)

2 pt (1 lb/500 g) strawberries, stems removed and thickly sliced (about 3 cups/12 oz/375 g)

1 lb (500 g) rhubarb, trimmed and cut into ¾-inch (2-cm) pieces (about 3 cups/12 oz/375 g)

1 teaspoon peeled and grated fresh ginger

1 teaspoon grated orange zest

1 cup (8 oz/250 g) sugar

¼ cup (1 oz/30 g) cornstarch (cornflour)

1 egg white, lightly beaten with a few drops of water until slightly foamy

1 tablespoon unsalted butter, cut into small pieces (optional)

Make this pie, the first fruit pie of the summer, when the rhubarb stalks are young and slender and the berries are irresistibly ripe. For a special treat, serve it with vanilla or Ginger-Honey Ice Cream (page 128).

1. Prepare the pastry dough and chill as directed.

2. Position a rack in the lower third of the oven and preheat the oven to 425°F (220°C).

3. On a lightly floured work surface, roll out the larger pastry disk into a 13-inch (33-cm) round about ⅛ inch (3 mm) thick. Drape the round over the rolling pin and carefully transfer it to a 9-inch (23-cm) pie dish, easing it into the bottom and sides. Trim the overhang to ½ inch (12 mm). Roll out the remaining pastry disk in the same way and carefully transfer it to a baking sheet. Place both crusts in the refrigerator.

4. In a large bowl, combine the strawberries, rhubarb, ginger, and orange zest. Toss to mix well. In a small bowl, stir together the sugar and cornstarch until the mixture is free of lumps. Add the sugar mixture to the fruit mixture and toss to combine.

5. Remove the pie dish from the refrigerator and brush the bottom and sides of the pie crust with the egg white. Spoon the fruit mixture evenly into the dish. Dot the surface with the butter, if using. Place the top crust over the fruit and trim the edges to leave a ¾-inch (2-cm) overhang. Fold the edge of the top crust under the edge of the bottom crust, then crimp the edges attractively to seal. Using a sharp knife, cut a few vents in the top crust. Set the pie on a baking sheet to catch any spills.

6. Bake the pie until the crust is golden and the filling is bubbling visibly through the vents, about 40 minutes. Transfer the pie to a rack and let cool for at least 1 hour before serving.

SERVES 8

NUTRITIONAL ANALYSIS PER SERVING
Calories 483 (Kilojoules 2,029); Protein 6 g; Carbohydrates 73 g; Total Fat 19 g;
Saturated Fat 9 g; Cholesterol 31 mg; Sodium 157 mg; Dietary Fiber 3 g

Pumpkin Molasses Doughnuts

4 cups (1¼ lb/625 g) all-purpose (plain) flour

2 teaspoons baking powder

½ teaspoon baking soda (bicarbonate of soda)

1 teaspoon salt

½ teaspoon freshly grated nutmeg

2 whole eggs, plus 1 egg yolk

¾ cup (6 oz/185 g) granulated sugar

⅓ cup (3½ oz/105 g) molasses

¾ cup (6 fl oz/180 ml) buttermilk

2 tablespoons unsalted butter, melted and cooled

½ cup (4 oz/125 g) pumpkin purée

peanut oil or solid vegetable shortening for deep-frying

confectioners' (icing) sugar

There are varying accounts of how New Englanders have come to love doughnuts, but there's no denying that these wonderful deep-fried "nuts" of dough are a favorite treat.

1. In a bowl, stir together the flour, baking powder, baking soda, salt, and nutmeg. Set aside. In a large bowl, using an electric mixer set on medium speed or a whisk, beat together the eggs, egg yolk, granulated sugar, and molasses. Add the buttermilk, butter, and pumpkin and beat until combined. Stir the flour mixture into the egg mixture, being careful not to overwork the dough. It will be very soft. Cover and refrigerate for 1–3 hours.

2. Pour oil to a depth of 2–3 inches (5–7.5 cm) into a deep, heavy sauté pan and heat to 365°F (185°C) on a deep-frying thermometer. (Or use enough shortening to equal that depth.) Meanwhile, transfer half of the dough to a lightly floured work surface and pat it out ½ inch (12 mm) thick. Using a floured 3-inch (7.5-cm) doughnut cutter, cut out as many doughnuts as possible and transfer them, along with the holes, to a sheet of waxed paper to rest for 5 minutes before frying. Gather the scraps and reroll them to cut out more doughnuts. Repeat the process of patting out and cutting out with the second half of the dough.

3. Lower the doughnuts, a few at a time, into the hot oil or shortening. After about 1 minute, they will rise to the surface and become well browned on the bottom. At this point, flip them with tongs or a slotted spoon and continue to fry until evenly browned on both sides, 1–3 minutes total. The outsides will become rather dark. Using the tongs or slotted spoon, transfer the doughnuts to paper towels to drain. Fry the remaining doughnuts and holes in batches, making sure the fat returns to 365°F (185°C) before adding the next batch.

4. Let the doughnuts cool for a moment. Then, using a sieve, dust the doughnuts with confectioners' sugar. Serve within 2 hours.

MAKES ABOUT 2 DOZEN 3-INCH (7.5-CM) DOUGHNUTS AND HOLES

NUTRITIONAL ANALYSIS PER DOUGHNUT
Calories 186 (Kilojoules 781); Protein 3 g; Carbohydrates 29 g; Total Fat 6 g; Saturated Fat 2 g; Cholesterol 29 mg; Sodium 180 mg; Dietary Fiber 1 g

Strawberry Shortcakes

3 pt (1½ lb/750 g) strawberries, stems removed and thickly sliced

¼ cup (2 oz/60 g) sugar, or to taste

1½ cups (12 fl oz/375 ml) heavy (double) cream

BISCUITS

1½ cups (7½ oz/235 g) all-purpose (plain) flour

3 tablespoons sugar

2 teaspoons baking powder

½ teaspoon baking soda (bicarbonate of soda)

¼ teaspoon salt

6 tablespoons (3 oz/90 g) chilled unsalted butter, cut into small pieces

¾ cup (6 fl oz/180 ml) buttermilk

The first building constructed in the harbor town of Portsmouth, New Hampshire, was on a long, low hill known as Strawberry Banke, for the acres of wild strawberries found there. Strawberries remain an early summer treat in Portsmouth, where they often are prepared with sweet buttermilk biscuits and whipped heavy cream.

1. Preheat the oven to 425°F (220°C). In a bowl, toss together the strawberries and 2–3 tablespoons of the sugar, or to taste. Reserve the remaining sugar. Crush some of the berries with a wooden spoon to make a bit of juice. Cover and refrigerate for about 1 hour.

2. To make the biscuits, combine the flour, sugar, baking powder, baking soda, and salt in a food processor and process briefly to mix. Add the butter and pulse until the dough looks crumbly. Transfer to a bowl, add the buttermilk, and toss briefly with a rubber spatula until the dough is evenly moistened. Dump the dough out onto a lightly floured work surface and knead gently so that it holds together in a loose, rough shape. With floured hands, pat it into a rectangle or square ¾–1 inch (2–2.5 cm) thick. Trim the edges so that they are even, then cut the dough into 6 equal pieces. Arrange the pieces 2 inches (5 cm) apart on an ungreased baking sheet.

3. Bake the shortcakes until they just begin to brown, 12–14 minutes. Remove from the oven and transfer the shortcakes to a rack to cool.

4. While the shortcakes are cooling, in a bowl, whip the cream with the remaining sugar until it is fairly stiff. Cover and refrigerate until needed.

5. Split each biscuit in half horizontally, and place the bottoms, cut sides up, on individual plates. Spoon the strawberries and juice onto the bottoms, dividing evenly. Top with the whipped cream and then put the biscuit tops in place. Serve immediately.

SERVES 6

NUTRITIONAL ANALYSIS PER SERVING
Calories 551 (Kilojoules 2,314); Protein 7 g; Carbohydrates 56 g; Total Fat 35 g; Saturated Fat 21 g; Cholesterol 114 mg; Sodium 421 mg; Dietary Fiber 4 g

ny gardener who has ever tilled a patch of soil in New England quickly learns one important truth: the growing season is remarkably short. Fortunately, the brief, cool summers provide the perfect climate for a plethora of berries, both wild and cultivated.

Of all the local berries, cranberries and blueberries have come to be most closely identified with New England because these two indigenous fruits were unknown to Europeans when they first set foot on American soil. Cranberries were discovered growing in bogs around Cape Cod, where they still flourish. Blueberries grew farther north on barren mountaintops and coastal islands. In addition, the region has always been rich with wild raspberries, huckleberries, and chokeberries, to name a few.

Today, the passage of summer can be marked by the berries available at the local pick-your-own farms and roadside stands. Bright, juicy strawberries appear in late June, followed by blueberries and raspberries. The season ends with deep purple blackberries and perhaps another round of plump fall raspberries. Some of the more enterprising farms, like Wilson Farms in Lexington, Massachusetts,

Local **Berries**

specialize in less common varieties, including gooseberries.

Despite the availability of cultivated berries, foraging remains a passion for many New Englanders who comb the roadsides and delve into deep woods for wild blueberries, brambleberries, barberries, cloudberries, and whatever else might make a tasty pie or preserve.

Apple-Raisin Bread Pudding

2 tablespoons unsalted butter

2 large tart apples such as Jonathan, Northern Spy, or Granny Smith, about 1 lb (500 g) total weight, peeled, halved, cored, and roughly chopped

2 tablespoons granulated sugar

4 whole eggs, plus 2 egg yolks

½ cup (3½ oz/105 g) firmly packed light brown sugar

1½ cups (12 fl oz/375 ml) milk

1½ cups (12 fl oz/375 ml) heavy (double) cream

2 tablespoons maple syrup

1 tablespoon bourbon whiskey

1 teaspoon vanilla extract (essence)

⅛ teaspoon salt

8 slices day-old white bread, ½ inch (12 mm) thick, crusts removed and bread torn into 1-inch (2.5-cm) pieces (about 7 cups/14 oz/440 g)

¾ cup (4 oz/125 g) raisins, soaked in hot water to cover for 30 minutes and drained

New England's repertoire of pudding recipes is long and varied: hasty pudding, bird's nest pudding, Indian pudding, popcorn pudding, summer pudding, and so forth. This cozy creation can be served plain or dressed up with a custard sauce or heavy cream.

1. Preheat the oven to 375°F (190°C). Butter a 2½-qt (2.5-l) soufflé or baking dish.

2. In a large frying pan over medium heat, melt the butter. Add the apples and granulated sugar and sauté, stirring often, until the apples are nicely glazed and most of the liquid has evaporated, 5–8 minutes. Remove from the heat and set aside.

3. In a large bowl, whisk together the whole eggs, egg yolks, and brown sugar until well mixed. Whisk in the milk, cream, syrup, bourbon, vanilla, and salt. Add the bread pieces and let them soak for 10–15 minutes. Stir in the apples and the drained raisins. Pour the mixture into the prepared baking dish.

4. Set the soufflé or baking dish in a larger roasting pan and place the pan on the center rack of the oven. Add hot water to the roasting pan to reach about halfway up the sides of the dish.

5. Bake the pudding until set and a knife inserted into the center comes out almost clean, 1–1½ hours. The timing will depend on the depth of the baking dish. Transfer the pudding to a rack to cool.

6. Serve the pudding warm or at room temperature.

SERVES 8

NUTRITIONAL ANALYSIS PER SERVING
Calories 539 (Kilojoules 2,264); Protein 11 g; Carbohydrates 65 g; Total Fat 27 g; Saturated Fat 15 g; Cholesterol 236 mg; Sodium 384 mg; Dietary Fiber 3 g

Blackberry Slump

2 pt (1 lb/500 g) blackberries

¾ cup (6 oz/185 g) sugar

¼ cup (2 fl oz/60 ml) fresh lemon juice

2 teaspoons grated lemon zest

BISCUITS

1 cup (5 oz/155 g) all-purpose (plain) flour

2 tablespoons sugar

1 teaspoon baking powder

¼ teaspoon baking soda (bicarbonate of soda)

pinch of salt

3 tablespoons unsalted butter, melted

½ cup (4 fl oz/125 ml) buttermilk

Slumps, grunts, buckles, and cobblers are all colonial desserts of fruit with a biscuit topping. What sets slumps apart, however, is that they are simmered on the stove top, rather than baked in the oven. Serve with heavy (double) cream, softly whipped cream, or vanilla ice cream.

1. To prepare the fruit, in a dutch oven or a wide, heavy saucepan with a tight-fitting lid, combine the berries, sugar, lemon juice, and lemon zest. (Heavy-duty aluminum foil will also work as a lid.) Set aside.

2. To make the biscuits, in a bowl, stir together the flour, sugar, baking powder, baking soda, and salt. Stir in the melted butter and buttermilk briefly to form a soft, lumpy dough.

3. Set the pan holding the berries over high heat, cover, and bring to a boil, stirring to ensure that the sugar dissolves. Reduce the heat to medium-low and drop spoonfuls of the biscuit dough onto the simmering fruit, spacing them evenly. Replace the cover and simmer gently until the biscuits are firm and dry to the touch, about 20 minutes. Avoid lifting the lid too frequently and allowing steam to escape.

4. Spoon the slump into warmed dessert bowls. A slump is unthickened, so a spoon is the best utensil for eating it.

SERVES 6

NUTRITIONAL ANALYSIS PER SERVING
Calories 314 (Kilojoules 1,319); Protein 4 g; Carbohydrates 62 g; Total Fat 6 g; Saturated Fat 4 g; Cholesterol 16 mg; Sodium 179 mg; Dietary Fiber 4 g

Ginger-Honey Ice Cream

2 cups (16 fl oz/500 ml) milk

2 cups (16 fl oz/500 ml) heavy (double) cream

1 piece fresh ginger, about 5 inches (13 cm) long, peeled and finely chopped (about ⅓ cup/2 oz/60 g)

1 cup (12 oz/375 g) mild honey, preferably wildflower or clover

8 egg yolks

¼ cup (1½ oz/45 g) finely chopped crystallized ginger

Because of such purveyors as Ben and Jerry's in Vermont, Steve's in Boston, and the Four Seas on Cape Cod, New England's ice cream is now legendary. Here's a grown-up flavor that combines the sweet perfume of local wildflower honey with the warm bite of fresh ginger.

1. Rinse a heavy saucepan with water and leave the inside slightly damp (this helps prevent the milk and cream from scorching). Pour the milk and cream into the saucepan, add the fresh ginger, and place over medium heat. Heat just until small bubbles appear along the edges of the pan. Remove from the heat, cover, and let stand for 15 minutes. Add the honey and return to medium heat. Warm gently, stirring often to dissolve the honey. The honey may make the mixture appear curdled at this point. Don't worry; it will smooth out once you whisk it with the eggs. Remove from the heat.

2. In a large bowl, whisk the egg yolks until blended. Gradually whisk the hot milk mixture into the egg yolks. If some of the ginger has sunk to the bottom of the saucepan, discard it before continuing. Pour the egg-milk mixture back into the pan and place over medium-low heat. Cook, stirring gently with a wooden spoon, until the mixture thickens enough to coat the back of the spoon, 5–8 minutes. Do not let the custard boil, or it will curdle.

3. Pour the custard through a fine-mesh sieve into a bowl. Lay a sheet of plastic wrap directly on the surface of the custard and refrigerate until well chilled.

4. Remove the chilled custard from the refrigerator and stir in the crystallized ginger. Pour the custard into an ice-cream maker and freeze according to the manufacturer's instructions.

5. Spoon into small glass bowls or sundae glasses to serve.

MAKES ABOUT 1 QT (1 L)

NUTRITIONAL ANALYSIS PER ½-CUP (4-FL OZ/125-ML) SERVING
Calories 452 (Kilojoules 1,898); Protein 6 g; Carbohydrates 45 g; Total Fat 29 g; Saturated Fat 17 g; Cholesterol 303 mg; Sodium 66 mg; Dietary Fiber 0 g

Although ice cream has been around since ancient times, it wasn't until New Englanders got involved that the frozen confection became America's favorite dessert. In the early 1800s, a Bostonian by the name of Frederic Tudor earned the title Ice King for his enterprise of cutting large blocks of ice from winter lakes, storing them in sawdust, and shipping them to warmer climates throughout the year. Thanks to Tudor's New England ice blocks, ice cream could be made everywhere—and it was.

The next significant Yankee contribution to the history of ice cream came in 1856, when the White Mountain Company, a small family-run business in Nashua, New Hampshire, began to manufacture hand-cranked ice-cream freezers. While White Mountain did not invent the machine, they did perfect the design and quickly became the biggest name in the business. Today, the White Mountain ice-cream maker is still manufactured according to tradition, boasting a pine-wood freezer barrel and a dasher (the part that churns the ice cream) of cast iron and beechwood.

Such is the predominance of the White Mountain machine that it was

Ice **Cream**

the one chosen by Ben and Jerry in 1978 for their first ice-cream shop in a renovated gas station in Burlington, Vermont. This savvy pair has since moved on to larger quarters. But hand-cranked freezers, packed with ice and rock salt, are still the centerpieces for ice-cream socials, summer picnics, and community gatherings throughout the region.

Cranberry-Pear Crisp

3 cups (12 oz/375 g) fresh or frozen cranberries

3 ripe pears such as Bosc or Bartlett (Williams'), peeled, halved, cored, and chopped

½ cup (3 oz/90 g) golden raisins (sultanas), soaked in hot water to cover for 30 minutes and drained

½ cup (4 oz/125 g) granulated sugar

grated zest of 1 orange (about 2 teaspoons)

½ teaspoon vanilla extract (essence)

TOPPING

½ cup (1½ oz/45 g) old-fashioned or quick-cooking rolled oats

½ cup (3½ oz/105 g) firmly packed light brown sugar

½ cup (2 oz/60 g) chopped walnuts or almonds (optional)

¼ cup (1½ oz/45 g) all-purpose (plain) flour

½ teaspoon ground cinnamon

¼ teaspoon salt

6 tablespoons (3 oz/90 g) chilled unsalted butter, cut into ¼-inch (6-mm) pieces

In the early 1800s, cultivation of the indigenous wild cranberry began in the renowned cranberry bogs of Cape Cod, and the tart berries have been popular ever since. Although cranberries co-star with the Thanksgiving turkey, many local cooks sweeten them for pies, cakes, crumbles, and crisps.

1. Preheat the oven to 375°F (190°C). Butter a 2-qt (2-l) baking dish.

2. To prepare the fruit, in a large bowl, toss together the fresh or unthawed frozen cranberries, pears, drained raisins, granulated sugar, orange zest, and vanilla.

3. To make the topping, in a food processor, combine the oats, brown sugar, nuts (if using), flour, cinnamon, and salt. Pulse briefly to combine. Add the butter and pulse until the mixture starts to hold together.

4. Spoon the fruit mixture into the prepared baking dish and cover evenly with the topping. Press lightly to compact. Bake until the fruit is bubbly and the top is browned, 50–55 minutes.

5. Remove from the oven and serve warm or at room temperature.

SERVES 6–8

NUTRITIONAL ANALYSIS PER SERVING
Calories 358 (Kilojoules 1,504); Protein 3 g; Carbohydrates 66 g; Total Fat 11 g; Saturated Fat 7 g; Cholesterol 28 mg; Sodium 91 mg; Dietary Fiber 5 g

Maple Rum Custard

2 cups (16 fl oz/500 ml) light (single) or heavy (double) cream

3 whole eggs, plus 2 egg yolks

2 tablespoons sugar

½ cup (5½ fl oz/170 ml) maple syrup

2 tablespoons dark rum

whipped cream (optional)

In the seventeenth century, much of the New England economy depended on importing raw molasses and distilling it into what was known as New England rum. Although little rum is produced in the Northeast today, more rum is consumed per capita here than elsewhere in the country.

1. Preheat the oven to 300°F (150°C).

2. Rinse a heavy saucepan with water and leave the inside slightly damp (this helps prevent the cream from scorching). Pour the cream into the saucepan, place over medium heat, and heat until small bubbles appear along the edges of the pan. Remove from the heat.

3. In a bowl, whisk together the whole eggs, egg yolks, sugar, and maple syrup until just blended. Gradually whisk the hot cream into the egg mixture without making it too frothy. Stir the rum into the custard. Pour into a large measuring pitcher or bowl with a pouring lip. Divide the custard evenly among six ⅔–¾-cup (5–6–fl oz/160–180-ml) custard cups or ramekins. Set the cups in a roasting pan or baking dish and place it on the middle rack of the oven. Add hot water to the pan or dish to reach halfway up the sides of the cups.

4. Bake the custards until set but the center still jiggles slightly when a cup is shaken, about 50 minutes. Let the custards cool for about 20 minutes in the water bath. Remove the custards from the water bath and set on a rack.

5. Serve the custards while still slightly warm. Or let cool completely, cover with plastic wrap, refrigerate for up to 2 days, and serve chilled, with dollops of whipped cream, if desired.

SERVES 6

NUTRITIONAL ANALYSIS PER SERVING
Calories 298 (Kilojoules 1,252); Protein 6 g; Carbohydrates 25 g; Total Fat 20 g; Saturated Fat 11 g; Cholesterol 230 mg; Sodium 68 mg; Dietary Fiber 0 g

The majestic and stalwart sugar maple dominates the character and landscape of much of New England. These cherished trees can live for up to four hundred years and account for almost 25 percent of all the native trees in the region. Every autumn, a steady stream of "leaf peeping" tourists comes to view their flashy display of fiery red, orange, and yellow. Beyond their great beauty, sugar maples, also known as rock maples, are the source of pure maple syrup and maple sugar, fundamental ingredients in the local cuisine and economy.

Toward the end of the long northern winter, the sturdy sugar maple offers the earliest hope of spring when the sap, spurred by the first warm days of the season, rises from the frozen earth to fill collecting buckets and tanks. Then, for days and nights, wood smoke mingled with sweet steam pours forth from sugar shacks, as sugar makers—typically farmers welcoming a chance for income during the off-season— boil down the sap to produce exquisitely flavored maple syrup. It takes an average of forty gallons (160 l) of sap to produce one precious gallon (4 l) of syrup.

The Sugar **Maple**

Friends often gather to help with sugaring—the local term for making maple syrup—and to celebrate the season with a sugar-on-snow party. Bowls are filled with fresh snow or shaved ice, and then some of the boiling syrup is poured on top, making a chewy caramel confection. Sour dill pickles, old-fashioned doughnuts, and hot coffee are served alongside.

Blueberry Tea Cake

2 cups (10 oz/315 g) all-purpose (plain) flour

1 teaspoon baking powder

½ teaspoon baking soda (bicarbonate of soda)

¼ teaspoon salt

¼ teaspoon ground cardamom

2 eggs

1½ cups (10½ oz/330 g) firmly packed light brown sugar

½ cup (4 oz/125 g) unsalted butter, melted and cooled

2 tablespoons dark rum

½ teaspoon grated lemon zest

1 cup (8 oz/250 g) plain yogurt

1 pt (8 oz/250 g) blueberries, picked over

confectioners' (icing) sugar

The idea for this moist yellow cake comes from Sam Hayward, chef-owner of Portland, Maine's Fore Street Restaurant, a lively spot known for its contemporary regional fare. I ate Sam's version one summer afternoon following a tremendous clambake. It's also wonderful for afternoon tea.

1. Preheat the oven to 350°F (180°C). Butter and flour an 8-inch (20-cm) square baking dish.

2. In a bowl, stir together the flour, baking powder, baking soda, salt, and cardamom. Set aside.

3. In a large bowl, using an electric mixer set on medium-high speed, beat together the eggs and brown sugar until thick and fluffy. Using a wooden spoon, stir in the cooled butter, rum, and lemon zest.

4. Add the flour mixture in three batches to the egg mixture alternately with the yogurt, beginning and ending with the flour. Mix just until smooth. (You can also use the mixer for this step, setting it at the lowest speed possible.) Gently fold in the blueberries. Spread the batter in the prepared baking dish.

5. Bake the cake until a toothpick inserted into the center comes out clean, 50–60 minutes. Transfer to a rack and let cool completely.

6. Using a sieve, dust the cooled cake with confectioners' sugar. Cut into squares and serve directly from the baking dish.

SERVES 9–12

NUTRITIONAL ANALYSIS PER SERVING
Calories 347 (Kilojoules 1,457); Protein 5 g; Carbohydrates 56 g; Total Fat 12 g; Saturated Fat 7 g; Cholesterol 71 mg; Sodium 207 mg; Dietary Fiber 1 g

Gooseberry Fool

1 lb (500 g) gooseberries (about 3 cups)

2 tablespoons water

¾–1 cup (6–8 oz/185–250 g) sugar, or to taste

1 cup (8 fl oz/250 ml) heavy (double) cream, well chilled

¼ teaspoon vanilla extract (essence)

Residents of both Old and New England share a love of the tart, translucent green gooseberries that thrive in their similar cool climes. Gooseberries are at their peak in midsummer, but you can make this sublime and simple dessert with other berries or stone fruits by simply adding a little lemon juice and cutting back on the sugar.

1. Remove the stem and blossom ends from the gooseberries with your thumb and forefinger or a sharp paring knife. Put the berries and water into a large, heavy saucepan and place over medium heat. As the berries heat, crush them with a potato masher or wooden spoon, then cook, stirring and mashing frequently, until the berries are quite juicy and somewhat puréed, about 10 minutes. Stir in the sugar to taste, using the lesser amount if you like your desserts a little tart. Continue to simmer for 1–2 minutes longer.

2. Remove the pan from the heat and transfer the berries to a bowl. Let cool, cover, and refrigerate until well chilled, at least 3 hours.

3. In a chilled bowl, whisk the cream until soft peaks form. Stir the vanilla into the chilled gooseberries and then fold the whipped cream into the gooseberries just until mixed.

4. Spoon the mixture into champagne flutes, wineglasses, or small sundae glasses. Serve immediately or cover and refrigerate for up to 1 day.

SERVES 4–6

NUTRITIONAL ANALYSIS PER SERVING
Calories 358 (Kilojoules 1,503); Protein 2 g; Carbohydrates 50 g; Total Fat 18 g; Saturated Fat 11 g; Cholesterol 65 mg; Sodium 19 mg; Dietary Fiber 0 g

Glossary

Bluefish

A perpetual, hard-fighting challenge for New England anglers, these silvery-blue North Atlantic fish are prized for their tender, rich-tasting flesh. Bluefish are best grilled, broiled, or baked.

Buttermilk

The thick, tangy, butter-flecked liquid left as a by-product of churning butter, buttermilk has been a New England standby since the arrival of the Puritans. Today, most buttermilk for sale is cultured, that is, factory-made by fermentation. But commercial products nonetheless yield fine results in the many savory and sweet dishes that buttermilk enriches.

Cider, Hard Apple

Press the juice from New England's abundant apple crop and you get sweet cider. Leave that juice to ferment, its sugars transforming into alcohol (3 to 8 percent by volume) by the action of airborne yeasts, and it turns to hard cider, the region's most popular drink in colonial times. Alas, commercial New England hard cider is less common today, although many cider fans make it at home. French, English, or Canadian hard cider is a good substitute.

Common Crackers

A specialty of Vermont, these wheat crackers resemble jumbo oyster crackers but are crispier and puffier. In earlier times, the crackers were sometimes called Montpelier biscuits, for the state capital and its natural springs that supplied the water deemed crucial to the crackers' taste and texture. Boston crackers are similar. Although the crackers are often enjoyed on their own or alongside a bowl of chowder, they are also frequently crumbled for coating seafood or chicken or for adding to stuffings or meat loaves.

Corn

From summer into autumn, sweet corn is a quintessential New England crop, at its best and sweetest freshly picked, before the sugar in the kernels can turn to starch. Two definitive regional ways to enjoy corn are among the simplest: boiled on the cob, right off the stalk, and slathered with butter; or scraped from the cob, enriched with cream and butter, seasoned with salt and pepper, and baked as a corn pudding.

Grapes, Concord

This beloved American grape variety, introduced in Concord, Massachusetts, in 1849, is distinguished by its deep blue color and rich, sweet flavor. Concord grapes are wonderful eaten out of hand or used for making juice, jellies, or jams.

Lobster

The cold waters of New England's rocky shoreline provide an ideal habitat for these large, big-clawed, meaty crustaceans known as the American or Northern lobster. The dark, blue-black shell turns a familiar "lobster red" when cooked by boiling or, as in a traditional clambake, steaming. For the best taste and texture, buy live lobsters, cooking them at home shortly before they are served. Those harvested in winter have greater quantities of firmer meat. Summer lobsters have softer flesh and a sweeter flavor.

Madeira

This rich-tasting fortified wine is available in five styles corresponding to sweetness: dry Sercial, medium-dry Verdelho and Rainwater, medium-sweet Bual, and sweet Malmsey. Named for the Portuguese island where it is produced, Madeira was a popular drink in colonial New England and is still used today in both savory and sweet dishes. Dry, medium-dry, or sweet sherries, traditional Spanish fortified wines, may be substituted in most cases.

Molasses

New England colonial traders brought home this dark, thick, sticky by-product of sugar processing from the West Indies, and its rich flavor and syrupy consistency, not to mention its economical price, won favor in the region's kitchens. Molasses still sweetens many traditional dishes, from baked beans to cookies. Light molasses results from the first boiling of the syrup, and dark molasses from the second. Blackstrap molasses, the darkest of all, has a distinctive hint of bitterness to complement its sweetness.

Mushrooms

Whether fresh or dried, wild or cultivated, mushrooms are a popular ingredient in New England cooking. From the woods come the **morel,** a meaty mushroom with a conical, dark brown, honeycombed cap; and the **chanterelle,** with its subtle flavor, golden color, and distinctive trumpet shape. The most common specialty mushrooms sold in markets are the **cremini,** resembling the familiar white button mushroom in size and shape but with a brown cast and a richer flavor; the **portobello,** a mature cremini with a broad, flat cap and a meaty taste and texture; and the **shiitake,** a full-flavored mushroom with a dark, curled cap and tough stem.

Mussels

An abundance of mussel beds is found along New England's crenulated shoreline, on its dock pilings, and in its estuaries. The common mussels found in New England have blue-black shells and tender, sweet-tasting pinkish brown flesh. While mussels are still caught from the wild, most mussels in the marketplace now come from a thriving mussel-farming

Herbs

BAY LEAVES
Pungent and spicy, the dried whole leaves of the bay laurel tree are used to flavor simmered dishes, marinades, and pickling mixtures.

CHERVIL
This fresh herb has leaves resembling a pale, lacey form of flat-leaf (Italian) parsley. Chervil adds a subtle flavor resembling parsley and anise to eggs, creamy cheeses and sauces, seafood, chicken, and vegetables.

CHIVES
A relative of the onion, this grasslike herb has a mild, sweet taste reminiscent of the pungent bulb. Fresh chives go well with eggs, cream cheeses, vegetables, soups, and salads.

DILL
Popular today from Eastern Europe to Scandinavia, this feathery-leaved herb has a sweet, aromatic flavor well suited to pickling brines, vegetables, seafood, chicken, veal, and pork. It is used fresh and dried.

MARJORAM
More delicately flavored than oregano, its close relative, although still pungent and aromatic, marjoram is used dried or fresh to season meats (especially lamb), poultry, seafood, vegetables, and eggs.

PARSLEY, FLAT-LEAF (ITALIAN)
This widely popular, fresh-tasting herb of southern European origin has a deeper, more complex flavor than the more familiar curly parsley, which is generally employed as a garnish.

ROSEMARY
This Mediterranean herb, used fresh and dried, has a strong, pleasantly resinous flavor well suited to lamb, veal, poultry, seafood, and vegetables.

SAGE
Popular throughout Europe, North Africa, and the Middle East, this pungent, mildly camphorous herb goes particularly well with fresh or cured pork, lamb, veal, or poultry. It is used fresh and dried.

TARRAGON
Fragrant and distinctively sweet with hints of anise, tarragon, whether used fresh or dried, complements salads, chicken, eggs, and vegetables.

THYME
This small-leaved herb of Mediterranean origin has a clean, aromatic character that adds flavor to many poultry, light meat, seafood, and vegetable dishes. It is used fresh and dried.

industry. Cultivated mussels tend to have a more delicate flavor, thinner, shinier black shells, and less sand or grit to deal with than their wild counterparts. Before cooking, mussels must be debearded, that is, the tough filament by which they cling to surfaces must be pulled off. On cultivated mussels, the beards tend to be very small and easy to remove. When cleaning mussels, discard any that do not close when tapped.

Oysters

Plump, sweet oysters may be found in various spots along New England's coastline. These Atlantic oysters vary in shape and size and usually take their names from the places where they are harvested, such as **Bristol,** Maine; **Chatham** and **Wellfleet,** both on Cape Cod in Massachusetts; and **Malpeque,** after the bay of the same name that laps Canada's Prince Edward Island. There is also a variety of flat or plate oyster from Maine known as **Belon** because of its similarity to the famed French variety. Oysters may be purchased live in the shell—best eaten on the half shell—or already shucked—best for cooked dishes such as pies and stews.

Peas

English peas, the familiar springtime and summer variety shelled fresh from their plump pods, were first planted in New England in 1602, on the tiny island of Cuttyhunk, near Martha's Vineyard in Massachusetts. They remain a favorite. Gaining popularity in recent years is the **sugar snap,** prized for its sweetness and the edibility of its crisp-tender pods.

Potatoes

Early in the eighteenth century, potatoes were first planted in Massachusetts and New Hampshire, eventually becoming important commercial crops. Potatoes

are still grown throughout New England, and some popular varieties include white, all-purpose **Maine** or **kennebec;** buttery-tasting **Yukon golds;** small **red potatoes,** at their best when harvested as immature new potatoes in the spring and early summer; **russets,** the familiar grainy-textured, flavorful baking potatoes; and waxy **white boiling potatoes,** ideal for steaming, roasting, or mashing.

Rhubarb

With its broad green leaves and its stalks resembling large pink celery, rhubarb, also known as pieplant, has long been a staple of New England gardens, growing readily and providing a bumper yield in spring and early summer. Its harvesttime and its tart flavor combine to make it an ideal partner to strawberries in traditional strawberry-rhubarb pies, jams, and sauces. The leaves, toxic in some plants, must be completely trimmed away.

Root Vegetables

Hardy root vegetables, which grow easily in cold climates and store well in cellars for winter, have long been staples of the New England diet, often appearing in such regional specialties as boiled dinners. Among these are **celeriac,** also known as celery root, the knobby root of a species of celery, with that vegetable's refreshing flavor; the sweet-tasting **parsnip,** which first came to America from Europe in the early seventeenth century and resembles an ivory-colored carrot; and the **rutabaga,** a large, yellow-fleshed type of turnip, enjoyed for its earthy flavor.

Rum, Dark

Some of the molasses brought home from the West Indies by New England traders was distilled to make rum, which remains a popular regional flavoring. Dark rums,

also known as Demerara rums, carry some of the caramel color and robust taste associated with molasses.

Salt Cod

The economy of colonial New England thrived on its cod-fishing industry, so much so that a cod appears on the Massachusetts state seal. Much of that long-ago catch was preserved as salt cod, which continues to be a regional staple. The fish are preserved first by gutting, filleting, and salting them at sea and then by sun-drying, resulting in a briny flavor and, after cooking, a tender, meaty texture. Before use, salt cod must be soaked to rehydrate the fish and reduce its saltiness. Salt cod is used in such regional specialties as fried salt cod cakes and balls.

Sardines

Maine is America's leading source of these slender, silvery members of the herring family. In springtime, they may be enjoyed freshly caught, simply cooked with tomatoes, fried, or grilled. At other times of year, sardines are available in their ubiquitous canned form.

Sausages

Long ago, European immigrants arrived in New England with recipes for their national sausages, which have since become established features of the region's cuisine. **Italian fresh sausages,** traditionally made from pork but now also available using lower-fat turkey or chicken, are available in two styles: sweet, usually scented with fennel seed, and hot, flecked with dried red chile. **Kielbasa** is a favorite Polish sausage made from pork and sometimes beef or veal, and is sold in more up-to-date turkey varieties as well. Its long links are most often smoked and precooked before sale. **Linguiça,** which gets its descriptive name from the Portuguese for "tongue," is a long, dry, coarse-textured cured sausage made from pork shoulder seasoned with garlic and paprika.

Scallops

With their distinctive scallop-edged shells, these mollusks are prized for the sweet, tender flesh of the ivory-colored, disk-shaped muscles that hold their shell halves together. The two most common types in New England are tiny **bay scallops,** primarily pulled from the waters off Cape Cod, and large, deep-water **sea scallops.**

Squashes

Long before Europeans came to New England, native tribes planted a wide variety of squashes. Later settlers adopted these vegetable-fruits as their own, making them staples of the New England diet. The warm months see the ripening of tender-skinned varieties such as the green, cylindrical **zucchini** (courgette), of which the delicate blossoms may also be eaten, usually stuffed and fried; and the similarly shaped, mild-flavored yellow **summer squashes.** Autumn brings orange-fleshed winter squashes, whose hard shells allow them to be kept throughout the cold months. Some of the most common varieties are the **acorn,** with a dark green, deeply ribbed shell and sweet flesh; the **butternut,** a large, tan-shelled, elongated variety enjoyed for its intense flavor; the succulent **Hubbard,** with its bumpy blue-green shell, often sold cut into smaller pieces; and the round, gray-green **kabocha.** The popular **pumpkin,** of which many types exist, has surprisingly bland, watery flesh, making many of them unsuitable for making pumpkin pie. The best pumpkins for this purpose are **sugar pumpkins,** which have a sweet flavor and light texture.

Spices

ALLSPICE BERRIES
Sweet Caribbean spice with a flavor suggesting a medley of cinnamon, cloves, and nutmeg.

CAYENNE PEPPER
Hot dried chile peppers ground to a fine red powder.

CINNAMON
Popular sweet spice derived from the aromatic bark of a type of evergreen, sold as whole dried strips—cinnamon sticks—or ground.

CORIANDER SEEDS
Small, citrusy, sharp-tasting seeds of the coriander plant. Used whole or ground as a seasoning.

CUMIN SEEDS
Strong, aromatic, dusky-tasting Middle Eastern spice, sold either as whole, small, crescent-shaped seeds or ground.

CURRY POWDER, MADRAS
Each region of India seasons its signature dishes with unique blends of spices, known and sold generically as curry powders outside of India. Those in the style of Madras, on the southeastern coast, often heavily favor coriander, along with cumin, black peppercorns, turmeric, black mustard seeds, chili powder, and ginger.

NUTMEG
The hard fruit pit of the tropical nutmeg tree, this popular warm, sweet baking spice may be bought already ground or, for fresher flavor, whole, to be grated as needed.

PAPRIKA, SWEET
Derived from dried paprika pepper, this powdered spice, popular in several European cuisines, delivers a sweet, earthy flavor to dishes. Paprika is also available in medium-hot and hot forms. Although Hungarian paprika is considered the best, Spanish paprika is a good substitute.

PEPPERCORNS
The most common of all savory spices is best purchased as whole peppercorns, to be crushed or ground as needed. Pungent black peppercorns are slightly underripe pepper berries whose hulls have oxidized during drying. Hotter white peppercorns come from fully ripened, husked berries.

RED PEPPER FLAKES
These coarsely ground flakes of dried red chiles are used to add moderately hot flavor to a range of dishes.

Index

Acknowledgments

Molly Stevens wishes to thank Annie Copps, Vinna Dunn, Sam Hayward, and Amy Trubek.

Leigh Beisch wishes to thank Vermont Country Naturals, Charlotte, VT; Flag Hill Farms, Vershire, VT; Butterwork Farms, Westfield, VT; Catamount Brewing, White River Junction, VT; and Fillamento, San Francisco, CA.

Weldon Owen wishes to thank the following people and associations for their generous assistance and support in producing this book: Desne Border, Ken DellaPenta, Dana Goldberg, Chris Hemesath, Annette Sandoval, Kate Sullivan, and Hill Nutrition Associates.

Photo Credits

Weldon Owen wishes to thank the following photographers and organizations for permission to reproduce their copyrighted photographs:
(Clockwise from top left) Pages 14–15 : Greig Cranna/The Picture Cube; Erik Rank; Jeff Greenberg/Index Stock;
Dana Gallagher; Kindra Clineff/The Picture Cube; Melanie Acevedo; Michael Melford
Page 16: George Mattei/Envision; Erik Rank; Ben Fink; Jeff Greenberg/Index Stock; Leigh Beisch
Page 46: John Kernick; Erik Rank; J.B. Marshall/Envision; Erik Rank (grazing cow)
Page 88: Erik Rank; Erik Rank; Dana Gallagher; Erik Rank
Page 116: Erik Rank; Richard Bowditch; Jean Higgins; Erik Rank; J.B. Marshall/Envision

Time-Life Books is a division of Time Life Inc.

Time-Life is a trademark of Time Warner Inc., and affiliated companies.

TIME LIFE INC.

President and CEO: **Jim Nelson**

TIME-LIFE TRADE PUBLISHING

Vice President and Publisher: **Neil Levin**

Senior Director of Acquisitions
and Editorial Resources: **Jennifer L. Pearce**

WILLIAMS-SONOMA

Founder and Vice-Chairman: **Chuck Williams**

Book Buyer: **Cecilia Michaelis**

WELDON OWEN INC.

Chief Executive Officer: **John Owen**

President: **Terry Newell**

Chief Operating Officer: **Larry Partington**

Vice President International Sales: **Stuart Laurence**

Associate Publisher: **Val Cipollone**

Editor: **Sarah Lemas**

Copy Editor: **Sharon Silva**

Consulting Editor: **Norman Kolpas**

Design: **Jane Palecek**

Production Director: **Stephanie Sherman**

Food Stylist: **Dan Becker**

Prop Stylist: **Sara Slavin**

Studio Assistant: **Sheri Giblin**

Food Styling Assistant: **Michael Procopio**

Scenic Photo Research: **Caren Alpert**

The Williams-Sonoma New American Cooking Series conceived and produced by Weldon Owen Inc.
814 Montgomery Street, San Francisco, CA 94133

In collaboration with Williams-Sonoma
3250 Van Ness Avenue, San Francisco, CA 94109

Separations by Bright Arts Graphics (S) Pte. Ltd.
Printed in Singapore by Tien Wah Press (Pte.) Ltd.

A WELDON OWEN PRODUCTION

First printed in 2000
10 9 8 7 6 5 4 3 2 1

Library of Congress
Cataloging-in-Publication Data

Stevens, Molly.
New England / general editor, Chuck Williams; recipes and
text, Molly Stevens; photography, Leigh Beisch.
p. cm. — (Williams-Sonoma New American Cooking)
Includes index.
ISBN 0-7370-2044-X
1. Cookery, American--New England style. I. Williams,
Chuck. II. Title. III. Series.
TX715.2.N48 S75 2000
641.5974— dc21 00-024943
CIP

A NOTE ON NUTRITIONAL ANALYSIS

Each recipe is analyzed for significant nutrients per serving. Not included in the analysis are ingredients that are optional or added to taste, or are suggested as an alternative or substitution either in the recipe or in the recipe introduction. In recipes that yield a range of servings, the analysis is for the middle of that range.

A NOTE ON WEIGHTS AND MEASURES

All recipes include customary U.S. and metric measurements. Metric conversions are based on a standard developed for these books and have been rounded off. Actual weights may vary.